MARY EMMERLING'S
AMERICAN COUNTRY

Details

MARY EMMERLING'S
AMERICAN COUNTRY

Details

text by **CAROL SAMA SHEEHAN**

design by **MAGGIE HINDERS**

CLARKSON POTTER/PUBLISHERS

NEW YORK

also by MARY EMMERLING

American Country
Collecting American Country
Mary Emmerling's American Country West
Mary Emmerling's American Country Cooking
Mary Emmerling's American Country Hearts
Mary Emmerling's American Country South
American Country Christmas
Mary Emmerling's American Country Classics
Mary Emmerling's American Country Gardens
Mary Emmerling's American Country Flags
Mary Emmerling's At Home in the Country
Mary Emmerling's American Country Christmas List Book
Mary Emmerling's American Country Cottages

Library of Congress Cataloging-in-Publication Data
Emmerling, Mary.
[American country details]
Mary Emmerling's American country details / by Mary Emmerling; text by Carol Sama Sheehan;
Includes index.
1. Decoration and ornament—United States. 2. Interior decoration—United States—History—20th century. I.
Sheehan, Carol Sama. II. Title. III. Title: American country details.
NK2002.E468   1994
747.213—dc20   94-641
ISBN 0-517-58369-0
10 9 8 7 6 5 4 3 2 1
First Edition

To my mother, and to my brother, Terry, who has
helped me move my decorating details from home to home.
Thank you.

acknowledgments

American Country Details is the continuation of all the travels I began with *American Country* in 1980.

This book is like twenty years of homes I have been in, friends I have met, photographers I have worked with, and new homes I have enjoyed lately.

Asking permission during these years to come into your homes and lives has been a delicate matter—but all of you have always been gracious and wonderful. My dearest thanks and love to all who have welcomed us.

While working on this book, I realized how much I need one like it, too—for all the houses I do, for the projects I work on, and for just opening my eyes to new ideas. Throughout the years I have heard the same questions over and over again from friends and readers: What do I do with my mantel? What should my flowers be put in? Where should I put my collections of china, dolls, and bears? Should I hang a quilt over my bed? Can I use an old door on my closet? I hope *Details* answers these questions and others you haven't even thought of yet.

I thank all of those who've allowed me to pull these details together: Joshua Greene, whose extraordinary talents as a photographer help me with all my books; the other photographers who filled in the ideas that were missing: Langdon Clay, Lisl Dennis, John Hall, Jeff McNamara, Chris Mead, Tim Street Porter, Jeremy Samuelson, Michael Skott, and Keith Trumbo.

A special thanks to the many friends, artists, decorators, and architects who assisted me so generously and made this book possible: Jimmie Cramer and Dean Johnson; Doug Cramer; Rogers Memorial Designer Showhouse, Southampton, Long Island, summer 1993; Ron and Marilyn Kowaleski; Susan Parrish; Tom and Claire Callaway; Fort Solanga, Long Island Showhouse 1991; Barbara Grants; Ann Fox Foley; Carol and Terry Shoppe; Nancy Reynolds; Dub and Bobbie King; Joanne Creveling; Conner Prairie Museum, Indiana; Skip and Olga Bowles; Sandy and John Hornitz; Andrea Dern; Salli Lagrone; Monica Greenberg; Winedale Museum; Bonnet House, Fort Lauderdale; Ellen O'Neill; Susie Burmann; Linda Cheverton; Jay Cobb; Trish Foley; Patti Kenner; and Peri Wolfman and Charles Gold.

My sincere thanks and love to Lauren Shakely for her guidance. And much gratitude as well to Maggie Hinders and Howard Klein; Hilary Bass, who is always there for me on all projects, travel, and favors; and everyone else at Clarkson Potter for their assistance, especially Mark McCauslin and Joan Denman.

To Carol Sheehan again and again, who puts the words in my mouth. To Melissa Crowley, who is there for me in all my projects, and to Janet Norales, for her help on the directory. To Jonathan and Samantha, who have put up with all our moving of our favorite decorating details.

And to my agents, Gayle Benderoff and Deborah Geltman, who are always there to get things done.

Enjoy and Happy Decorating,

Mary Emmerling

contents

introduction

Decorating a home, to me, is an art, not a science. When I bring fabrics, furnishings, folk art, and collections together in a room, my first consideration is intuitive. How do things look? What feels out of place? What if I moved the sofa there, hung the mirror here, changed the Navajo rug for sisal, put up my spongeware, and brought out my English blue-and-white china for the corner cupboard? I experiment in every room, trying to avoid preconceived notions of what is supposed to go where, and I make the rules up as I go along, looking for an arrangement that is pleasing, comfortable, and spontaneous.  The trend in home decoration today is away from uniformity and formality and toward an eclectic but practical

mixture of styles and periods. It depends on seeing things with a fresh eye and not being afraid to express personal style.

Details is designed to help you see anew the elements of home design and to offer a handful of solutions for every possible challenge that comes your way as you assemble a satisfying look for your house and garden. My experience in decorating my own home and the homes of friends and clients over the years has convinced me that the more you see, the more you learn. That's why I isolated decorative treatments by category, ranging from Architectural Elements to Windows, permitting you to browse and compare among hundreds of examples. This is exactly how I go about my business—identifying specific

treatments as I encounter them, and filing away the ones that would be successful in other settings, too.

You'll see that I am a great believer in assigning unexpected roles to things. It's fine to use an old painted bench for seating, but it works wonderfully as a shelf for display. A printed kitchen tablecloth originally designed to add color to the daily meal can be recycled as a surprisingly effective window curtain. And while birdhouses and watering cans are associated with gardens, collections of them make pleasing arrangements inside, too.

Your own lifestyle will shape your personal decorating style. If you like to entertain friends around the kitchen table, with kids and dogs underfoot, your kitchen should reflect that attitude, perhaps with abundant ceramic bowls nesting in glass-front cabinets and simple tables with plenty of chairs. If lavish cocktail parties are your style, you will be happier with a house that welcomes friends with dramatic lighting and other elegant flourishes.

Obviously, your budget controls what you can and cannot do, to a certain extent. But the imaginative decorator can do amazing things with limited resources. For example, a plain wood floor painted to resemble marble can give a room a feeling of style and luxury at little cost.

Above all, I hope *Details* encourages you to look upon home decoration as an enjoyable and enriching experience. It's easier than you might think, and the rewards can be shared with everyone who is important to you.

archi-
tectural
elements,
floors &
stairs

Much as I admire old houses, I have often had to live in places that had less architectural character than I would have liked. Not everyone has a pilastered fireplace, a sweeping staircase, a high vaulted ceiling, or a rich parquet floor. Those who do should take advantage of these assets. A stairway, for example, offers a trip through the past when it is hung with family photographs and portraits. Taking into account any structural limitations, an architectural signature can be transformed by raising a ceiling to expose rustic beams, adding a chimney made with local stone, or installing a floor of decorative tile.

Floors, in fact, because they allow us to work with gravity instead of against it, are one of my favorite ways to dress up a house easily. A flair for the dramatic can be expressed just with the introduction of a large-scale element to entertain the eye, such as a freestanding column, an antique frieze, or a birdbath used as a plant stand.

PRECEDING PAGES: Visually interesting fragments, salvaged from other buildings, find new life in room interiors as decorative additions, while floor and stair treatments are integral parts of the house architecture. **LEFT:** The luxury of a spiral staircase, this one connecting three different wood floor treatments, is usually a feature of grand rather than modest houses since such complex features require space and expense. For a magnificent staircase like this one, very little embellishment is required. **ABOVE:** A plain wood floor becomes exciting when it is given a witty design showing the orientation of the house. **BELOW:** A dramatic room divider with a sculpted appearance adds interest and can be used to mount a favorite collection.

ABOVE: A towering chimney of native stone, a vaulted ceiling, and buttressed beams dominate this barnlike house. The plain ceiling fan helps to heat and cool the large open space. **BELOW:** Instead of a banister, this modern staircase offers a series of perches.

ABOVE: A fresh coat of paint can help to celebrate an outstanding stairway or bring stature to an undistinguished one. **BELOW:** The banister on this second-story landing was painted white to set it apart from the stained wood floor.

The ceiling in a tall, high-tech kitchen was brought down in scale with the installation of a stained wood box fabrication.

Taking its cue from the original beams and half-timbered walls, this elegant room radiates Tudor style and charm.

This dramatic Doric column, rescued from another building, adds its classical flair and dignity to a paneled room.

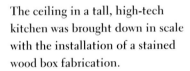

LEFT: The recesses built into the thick walls of most adobe houses provide their own architectural interest and offer a natural stage for display. RIGHT: An arched alcove leading from one room to another, painted and sparely decorated, makes a dramatic passageway.

A wood floor painted in a classic black-and-white checkerboard pattern has been treated with a faux marble finish to emphasize the formality of the look. The traditional floor treatment, which has been popular for centuries because it achieves an expensive look at minimal cost, works well with a variety of country and formal antiques.

Bricks, laid in a random pattern, add texture and color to a floor and, inevitably, a durable, rustic character. Indoors, brick may be finished with polyurethane to keep down brick dust and make cleaning easier, although some people prefer the matte look of plain brick. Flooring bricks are made especially for this purpose in different shapes and sizes.

Painted to resemble European tile patterns, this wood floor is a lively conversation piece exactly in keeping with the country furnishings in the room. Almost any tiled floor can be imitated in a painted version, and there are craftsmen who can adapt a pattern for your particular room. If you wish to try floor painting yourself, refer to one of the many excellent books available on the subject.

A trompe l'oeil triple play, this floor gives the impression that a stem of cherries has fallen onto a woven rug that sits on a painted floor. Stenciling and painting have often been used for effects that fool the eye. For those who love pattern but hate the turned-up edges and cleaning problems presented by carpets or carpeting, paint may be the best solution.

An intricate stenciled treatment, with a floral medallion as the central image, gives this floor the appearance of handsome inlaid wood. Designs that play on the parqueted floor theme need a good wood floor as their base, since flaws will be more apparent.

A faux marble finish and border on a wood floor resembles a church mosaic that might have come from Renaissance Italy. The fancier a design and border, the more costly it will be to produce, but since the most elaborate borders may obviate the need for costly furnishings, the expense may be the best investment.

A painted zebra skin design lends an *Out of Africa* personality to this room. Only the plainest furnishings work well with a floor this exotically patterned.

An entryway, with its limited square footage, is a relatively simple floor to decorate. Here, beneath a birdbath plant stand, it is a surprising welcome mat for visitors.

To make this dining room floor as fancy as its furnishings, the surface was painted to resemble colored tiles with marble insets. The result is both austere and elegant.

LEFT: The stenciled border was inspired by a detail on the cabinet and harmonizes with the pattern in the needlepoint rug. **RIGHT:** A grapevine painted in the subtle wood hues of the flooring becomes a pleasant surprise underfoot.

A conventional staircase, painted to resemble stone steps, is paired with a mural depicting a storybook country house. The often lost wall space becomes a unified work of art.

The handiwork of a craftsman staircase dating from the early nineteenth century can be better appreciated when it is left free of most decoration.

Here architectural elements work in harmony, leading the eye up past the owner's collections through an asymmetrical doorway to the arched niche of the room beyond.

Painted Floor Treatments

Drab wood floors and out-of-date resilient flooring such as vinyl and linoleum can be given new life with painted patterns, a do-it-yourself project requiring only moderate effort and skills. Surfaces must be carefully prepared before paint can be applied. Remove wax with a heavy-duty wax remover, then lightly sand the floor. Clean thoroughly and seal the surface with floor varnish. A primer coat of oil-based paint creates a working surface, then the pattern can be painted freehand or using stencils. A final coat of varnish or polyurethane will help the new floor stand up to traffic.

Rustic painted stairs, railings, and a swinging gate (probably first installed to confine toddlers and pets) give a humble home an inviting entrance.

The spiral metal staircase, convenient when space is at a premium, has been dressed up with a painted landing. The feeling is of an old-fashioned lighthouse.

This original stairway owes its charm to its carved decoration and the weathered paint. Instead of slats or posts, the balustrade has a pierced design.

LEFT: A suspended marble staircase with brass handrail in a modern house provides an architectural spectacle from every level. Not everyone can afford this sort of lavish carpentry, but it shows what can be done when a staircase is left open. **RIGHT:** Painting this staircase in contrasting colors has allowed the period detailing to stand out.

The treads in a custom-made wrought-iron staircase coordinate with the pine flooring in the main room. Beyond, the fireplace treatment features steps of its own.

Collections of mirrors and watering cans are the dominant elements in the simple wooden stairway. White paint sets off a rag rug runner.

The installation of a Gothic arch, accentuated with white paint, turns a narrow staircase into an impressive passageway.

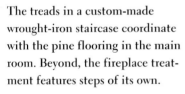

LEFT: The balusters and railings of this staircase have been embellished with ornate wrought-iron detailing. Wrought iron, a material developed for exterior detailing, provides support without blocking the view in its interior interpretations. **RIGHT:** A wood staircase with a traditional newel post shows off an unusual geometric treatment in its balustrade.

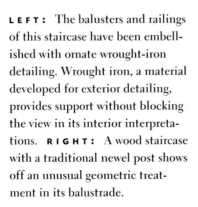

beds

There is no way of getting around it. The bed occupies center stage in every bedroom, and that is why it deserves special treatment, starting with the choice of bedstead. The old-fashioned romance of a lavishly canopied four-poster is hard to resist, especially when it offers the creature comforts of a feather bed and down pillows. But even the plainest bed can be dressed to the hilt, using antique linens, colorful quilts, lacy pillow shams, and flirtatious bed skirts, or dressed down, using layers of white for a simple effect. Beds with ornate headboards have a commanding presence. In lieu of headboards, Pendleton Indian blankets, boldly patterned patchwork, or appliquéd antique lace can achieve a similar effect. Decorative touches on and around the  bed contribute to the restful ambience: bouquets of fresh flowers, heaps of pillows and layers of throws, groupings of mirrors reflecting candlelight, and drawers lined with scented paper. In the most private chamber of the house, fantasy reigns supreme.

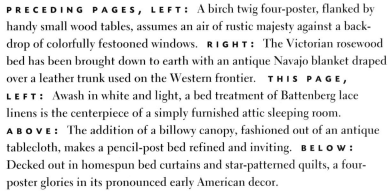

PRECEDING PAGES, LEFT: A birch twig four-poster, flanked by handy small wood tables, assumes an air of rustic majesty against a backdrop of colorfully festooned windows. RIGHT: The Victorian rosewood bed has been brought down to earth with an antique Navajo blanket draped over a leather trunk used on the Western frontier. THIS PAGE, LEFT: Awash in white and light, a bed treatment of Battenberg lace linens is the centerpiece of a simply furnished attic sleeping room. ABOVE: The addition of a billowy canopy, fashioned out of an antique tablecloth, makes a pencil-post bed refined and inviting. BELOW: Decked out in homespun bed curtains and star-patterned quilts, a four-poster glories in its pronounced early American decor.

ABOVE: In an antique-filled room, the rich colors and textures of old bed coverings and linens carry out the traditional period look in a carefully coordinated fashion. **BELOW:** The bold graphics of an antique Crown of Thorns quilt have been exploited to create a striking visual headboard on the chinked log wall behind the bed. A working fireplace is a romantic touch in any bedroom.

ABOVE: The iron bedstead was painted black, except for some brass detailing left exposed, to coordinate with the ebony wood furniture in the room. Custom-made bed curtains, hanging on a black rod framework, help to evoke the late-Victorian decorative theme, also evident in the red upholstered chair and the rose pattern rug. **BELOW:** This room has been sparsely furnished to permit the mammoth scale of the four-poster to be fully appreciated. The patchwork quilt adds a welcome dose of color.

ABOVE: Antique textiles are better seen than hidden away, as in this room, where one quilt dominates a wall and a host of others, in open storage in a corner cabinet, also show their colors. **BELOW:** When a white-only color scheme is studiously applied, the result can be dreamy, romantic, and serene. In keeping with the Victorian spirit of this room, the vanity is decorated with a crystal and silver dressing set.

ABOVE: The classic style of a unique painted bedstead is acknowledged in the choice of decorative accessories for the room, including tapestry pillows and prints celebrating the architecture of ancient times. **BELOW:** In a bedroom overlooking a verdant landscape, the bamboo bed has been dressed with vivid floral patterns and a canopy, improvised with a gauzy fabric, that spells tropical romance.

ABOVE: Taking its color cue from the painted head-board, this bedroom was papered to introduce pattern. **BELOW:** A highly coordinated ensemble of floral prints and images creates a sumptuous and very feminine bedchamber.

ABOVE: A sleeping cot suspended from ropes turns an ordinary bedroom into a seaworthy berth, complete with a porthole mirror, nautical sketches, and curtains running with fish. **BELOW:** The Casbah beckons in this exotic attic bedroom.

ABOVE: A sleigh bed becomes a stage for drama in a room with black skirting, pillow shams, and French country bedding. **BELOW:** A bed's graceful lines are accentuated with the addition of crochetwork on the canopy frame and a colorful appliquéd quilt.

ABOVE: When space permits, a bed can be floated in the middle of a bedroom, away from walls.
BELOW: Long panels of ticking fabric, knotted at the top, make a surprisingly elegant addition to a pencil-post bedstead.

A bed newly fashioned in the Craftsman style has been surrounded by an eclectic assemblage of art and antiques and dressed with a combination of paisley prints for a sophisticated, tailored look. The nineteenth-century American portrait, Oriental screen, and a hooked rug live amicably together because of the room's simplicity.

Shaker furniture remains an endless source of inspiration for decorators who believe utilitarian things can also be beautiful. The three beds were crafted by different carpenters and show distinguishing details, but all conform to the Shaker ethic of clean, simple lines with a minimum of ornamentation. Their bedcoverings are an unaffected combination of white spreads and blue-striped blankets that would go handsomely in a bedroom of today.

A four-poster bed is the classic showcase for a collection of antique coverlets and quilts, complemented by the Native American blanket on the wall. Sometimes a bedroom may seem too small to accommodate a large bed, but the contrast in scale may make the room seem grander than it is.

Even in a spacious, custom-decorated bedroom, the bed itself remains the center of interest, especially this four-poster formally outfitted with scalloped canopy, bed curtains, scalloped skirt, and upholstered mattress treatment. In such a room, the bed comes first and the rest of the room follows its lead.

A bedroom decorated to evoke the pleasures of life in a country cottage conveys the mix-and-match charm of a crazy quilt by bringing together the disparate patterns in bedding, rug, and wall covering. When the decorating style is meant to convey "cozy," the more elements and patterns the better.

The repetition of the swag of the window treatments in the mosquito netting canopy of the bed, and the palette of creams and neutrals in the curtains and bed fabrics, turn this bedroom into a genteel setting for rest and reflection. The pale tones are also augmented by the amount of natural sunlight streaming through the four windows.

bowls
&
baskets

If I have a decorating signature, it is bowls and baskets, jars and jugs—used to hold anything and everything. Containers originally designed for other purposes provide a surprisingly efficient and decorative alternative to drawers and bins for storing both the necessities of life, such as mail, fresh eggs, and toilet paper, and the indulgences, such as perfumes, fragrant soaps, and the latest compact discs. Rustic catchalls and carriers such as baskets, buckets,

bottle totes, crocks, and an almost infinite variety of bowls all can be enlisted into service around the house, often all the more welcome because they are portable. Whether containers are genuine antiques, reproductions, or simply tag sale bargains, they enliven every corner and tabletop where they are assigned duty. Neatness counts—especially when you've taken so much care to make your home beautiful. And attractive containers keep things organized and enhance the decor at the same time.

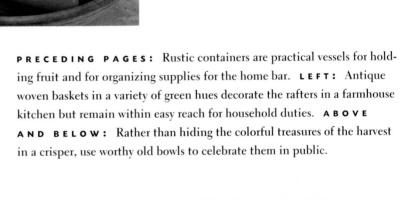

PRECEDING PAGES: Rustic containers are practical vessels for holding fruit and for organizing supplies for the home bar. **LEFT:** Antique woven baskets in a variety of green hues decorate the rafters in a farmhouse kitchen but remain within easy reach for household duties. **ABOVE AND BELOW:** Rather than hiding the colorful treasures of the harvest in a crisper, use worthy old bowls to celebrate them in public.

In a kitchen where wood surfaces predominate, a ceramic bowl filled with green apples and a woven basket containing peas ready for shelling add splashes of vivid color. Sometimes it's unnecessary to put away all the groceries. Fruits, vegetables, nuts, eggs, and other comestibles can be left out for a limited time without harm. Bowls and baskets allow fresh bounty to be enjoyed as a visual treat before it is put on the menu.

Cutting boards of all shapes and sizes are fun to collect but difficult to store neatly. Here they are kept at hand in a large splint basket. Old and new baskets can solve lots of storage problems in the kitchen, at the same time contributing a decorative effect. And they can be conveniently carried away when a surface is needed for food preparation.

An old dough bowl has been converted into a surprisingly effective centerpiece, using the ingredients of the fall harvest. Plain paper bags tied with raffia and bursting with nuts show the versatility of a common carrier for display. Surrounded with apples, this symbol of bounty would serve equally well on the kitchen counter or on the Thanksgiving table.

Potted primroses, dried herbs, and an abandoned bird's nest find a new home in a wood salad bowl. Large bowls are especially suitable for arrangements of natural objects, which can be changed with every season. In the spring there might be a grouping of crocuses (scattered with moss to conceal the plastic pots); in summer, seashells and stones.

Baskets and bowls become the dominant decorative element in a keeping room that dates from the time when these containers were the mainstays of domestic life. Today they are appreciated not only for their utilitarian value but for their beauty as handmade objects. In today's homes every inch of space is needed. Hanging baskets from the rafters frees other surfaces for work or storage.

Much of decorating has to do with the way we see and reinterpret what is already around us. Pottery, such as these Southwestern water jugs hammocked in rawhide, can and should be exhibited as authentic works of art, lending the richness of their patina and the magic of their tradition to any interior.

ABOVE: When not in use, handmade baskets arranged atop a country cupboard create a visual family of like forms. **BELOW:** A blue-and-white spatterware bowl, filled to the brim with summer pickings, makes a mouth-watering display for the table.

ABOVE: The wrought-iron plate holder extends storage capacity in a room while showing off, in this case, simple white bowls. **BELOW:** A silver bowl on a mirrored tabletop is filled with alabaster peaches and woodland potpourri.

ABOVE: Two forms of natural found objects, a bleached skull and pinecones collected in a wicker basket, come together to make a welcoming entranceway. **BELOW:** An antique colander, here with baby lettuces, can also serve as a fruit bowl or wall hanging.

ABOVE: The corner of a country porch has been decorated with a variety of natural materials, including a basket hung to function as a picture frame. **BELOW:** Even the workhorse bowl by the kitchen sink is a feast for the eye.

Not all bowls are circular. Heart-shaped containers, used here to hold cooking spices, have both emotional and visual appeal.

A multitiered wicker basket stand makes an attractive storage cupboard, containing its goods without hiding their natural beauty.

The wire mesh basket stand is the perfect in-and-out box for perishable items such as tomatoes and corn. Choice pieces of antique wire can still be found at tag sales.

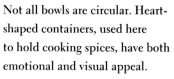

LEFT: The faded beauty of dried roses is well served by a venerable gathering basket, itself mellowed by time. **RIGHT:** Ceramic mixing bowls, beautiful in themselves, can be taken off the shelf at mealtime for use as unconventional serving dishes.

Everything from apples and oranges to favorite old photographs can be exhibited together in a decorative Victorian wire basket stand.

A grand old bowl with the quality of sculpture, set on a table made from a column topped with glass, adds a graceful note to a garden-green porch setting.

Bowls arranged in multiples can turn a simple table or countertop into a pleasing still life.

LEFT: Terra-cotta pots, ideal containers for growing herbs, lend themselves to other uses too. In this kitchen, wooden cooking utensils are organized and at hand.

RIGHT: A wire bottle carrier from the nineteenth century with unusually elegant lines converts into a service bar for mixers.

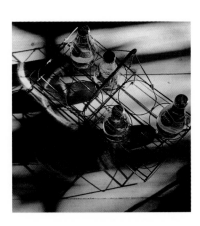

A basket holding bars of white soap becomes a decorative asset in the bathroom. A container filled with identical objects creates a different effect than one filled at random, conveying a sense of luxury even though the objects may be as mundane as toilet paper, cotton balls, or soap. Keeping everything out also lets you know at a glance when it is time to restock these essential items.

The portability of baskets makes them ideal for occasions such as picnics or beach parties, when supplies like plastic cups and cutlery and paper towels have to be transported to the scene. This basket even has a handle on trash disposal. For carrying picnic necessities, a square, deep basket works better than a round or oval shallow basket.

Some people collect colanders for their rustic charm as well as for their usefulness as decorative containers aound the house. The perforated construction allows ripe fruit and vegetables to be kept out longer without spoiling. Enameled metal is best for use with water.

A specimen antique yellow bowl has been assigned a prominent but secure place in the room, atop an old cupboard and out of harm's way. Its beauty alone justifies special treatment. The banded pattern of the bowl interplays with the carved decoration on the cupboard and the miniprint paper on the wall.

A large enamel bucket filled with ice becomes a serving bowl for a favorite summertime treat—a great way to serve the kids without opening the freezer door a dozen times. It could just as easily be used to chill wine or other beverages for a special occasion.

It's really impossible to have too many baskets. Here a colorful array functions as the produce bin for a kitchen with an overflow of freshly harvested herbs and vegetables. If baskets begin to crowd your kitchen, fill them with muffins or fresh-picked apples and give them away. Once basket giving becomes a tradition with your friends, you'll have a rotating supply.

chairs & sofas

It used to be that decorators and their clients believed a room looked messy and unfinished unless the furniture matched as a suite. To today's eye, an assortment of chairs and sofas reflecting contrasting periods and styles is far more inviting. Unmatched furniture is not only more casual but more fun, expressing the different facets of an owner's personality. There are many ways you can break out of the furniture-showroom look: add a rugged blanket to a sofa, or a homey quilt, or an exotic paisley spread as a throw. Slipcovers, plain or tight-fitting, loose or ruffled and tied with bows, give a welcome facelift to favorite upholstered pieces. Tassels, welting, and buttons are one-of-a-kind finishing touches.  Pillows allow the introduction of rich fabrics like damask and tapestry—and with them you can change a look in an instant. And straight chairs in different shapes and sizes, some painted, others with cushions, and still others left as is, add surprising interest to a room and, occasionally, can be the best seat in the house.

PRECEDING PAGES: Versatile country seating, with its distinctive decorative qualities, can be as pretty as a cushioned wicker sofa or as unadorned as a pair of rugged ladder-back chairs. **LEFT:** The attic room of a beach house is informally furnished with a set of balloon-back rattan chairs, while contrasting fabrics make a splash on the overstuffed sofa. **ABOVE:** A faded Indian blanket adds a touch of warmth and spontaneity when recruited to decorate a traditional wing chair. **BELOW:** Even outdoor seating can have flair.

This romantic, light-filled bedroom shows the advantage of furniture recycling. The chaise longue, which first came into vogue as a variant on the daybed in the late eighteenth century, gets a fresh start with a beautiful piece of lacy cutwork that originally graced a table. Two old chairs, one with cabriole legs, have been painted and reupholstered with new fabric.

The bathroom might be the last place anyone would expect to find upholstered seating, but it gives a sense of luxurious comfort to this modern home spa, countrified by the birchbark artwork on the wall and furnished with a simple daybed made inviting with throw pillows and an antique appliquéd quilt.

Even the formal living room can have personality with a few simple touches. A loosely slipcovered sofa takes the starch out of tradition without sacrificing style or comfort. Instead of stiff throw pillows with fabric that matches the sofa, a collection of vintage remnants has given each pillow a unique identity. Pillows are essential for comfort with nearly every kind of upholstered seating, no matter how well designed.

A luxuriant armed divan has been decorated to the hilt with pillows, fine fabrics, and fringe details, with a little gem of a chair brought alongside for company. Round and rectangular pillow shapes are cleverly alternated for interest. Diminutive chairs may be too small for adult guests, but they are pretty to look at and can double as side tables.

The camelback loveseat fits into the decorative scheme of a romantic cottage with its ruffled skirt, lacy scarf, and sham-covered pillows. The use of whites and off-whites on the sofa, instead of prints, allows pattern to be introduced elsewhere in the room in generous doses, as on the screen, table skirt, and upholstered armchair.

After a contemporary artist gets through with it, this mainstream suite of furniture from the 1950s rockets into the twenty-first century, ready to bring to the right room an unexpected fresh look. When haunting shops and flea markerts for secondhand upholstered furniture, check the overall form and condition of wood and springs first. The fabric can easily be replaced if the structure is sound.

ABOVE: An armchair smartly upholstered in ticking and given the pizzazz of Hawaiian printed fabrics makes an inviting corner in an island home.
BELOW: A miniature glider, once used as a salesman's sample, takes up little room on the porch.

ABOVE: Throwing convention to the winds, the owner of this elegant fauteuil used contrasting country fabrics, one homespun, the other floral, to create an original look. **BELOW:** Deck chairs once used aboard ocean liners are at home with a view of the pool.

ABOVE: The fancy French armchair, upholstered in a Provençal country print instead of silk brocade, projects a welcoming informality in its nook in the room. **BELOW:** Cushions and pillows and linens and lace create a setting for a Victorian lemonade party.

ABOVE: A scalloped linen scarf and a pillow covering with lace detail enhance the feminine personality of a petite slipper chair. **BELOW:** A set of rush-bottomed chairs was spruced up with pastel paint and slipcovers inspired by old seed packet designs.

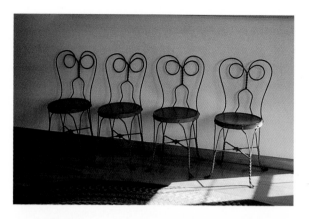

Vintage wire ice-cream parlor chairs with wooden seats have been lined up informally against a plain wall to heighten their sculptural qualities. Small chairs with interesting shapes are worth scouting for at barn sales and flea markets. They can be used to decorate a room's empty spaces, at the same time providing extra seating when needed. And chairs with hard, flat seats can double as side tables.

When porch furniture is chosen for its compatability with the architecture, a pleasing uniform scheme is the result. Log cabins and twig chairs have the same pioneer origins. The loveseat has the natural springiness of bentwood, but the cushions have been added to make them more comfortable and to add a dash of bright color to the surroundings.

Two well-made painted chairs, standing out in a room full of early American antiques, are decorative objects in themselves. The unusual corner chair is a two-way conversation piece. The chairs' open backs do not prevent the light from permeating the room.

An attic corner has been transformed into a mini-museum using chairs of different periods and different shapes, each bearing its own decorative element.

Even a humdrum flea market find like this upholstered chair from the 1940s, with casters, can enjoy a useful new life when dressed in a colorful crazy quilt slipcover.

An invitingly graceful Lloyd Loom wicker armchair needs no accessories to call attention to itself when set on the shingled porch of a Long Island country home.

LEFT: The upholsterer's art has made an elegant seat out of an ordinary divan, using rich velvet and such details as rope cording, buttoned bolsters, and the novel device of securing pillows with decorative wall hooks. **RIGHT:** Cording is used in a contrasting color to define the outlines of a plump armchair.

collec-
tions

Decorating with collections is one of the most effective and rewarding ways to stamp the home with a unique personal style. I move frequently, and I often have to leave furniture behind—or sell that old sports equipment at a tag sale—but I always take my collections with me. I could sleep on a mattress on the floor, but I wouldn't feel at home without my folk art. Objects that have been arranged to reflect a single theme, such as an array of hearts or watering cans, not only communicate a special passion to the onlooker, but add a commanding visual tableau to an interior. Walls, tabletops, shelves, and ledges all lend themselves to showing off cherished things. Collections may pay tribute to craftsmanship, or the appeal of exotica, or the artful side of household tools. Sometimes the most provocative collection is of ordinary family snapshots or travel souvenirs. Placed in old frames and sensitively arranged on a table or mantel, they can summon nostalgia even in people who aren't relatives or didn't make the trip!

PRECEDING PAGES: Any gathering of similar objects, whether an array of miniature landmarks or a litter of fabric felines, invites the eye to investigate and enjoy. **LEFT:** A collection of blue-and-white spatterware defines the personality of this country kitchen. **ABOVE:** Handmade water jugs and crocks have been purposefully arranged for a dramatic decorative effect. If the collection were dispersed, the casual viewer might fail to take notice of the exceptional craftsmanship represented. **BELOW:** Recycled fishing bobs make a colorful outdoor wall.

Glitter fruit is an unusual collectible that can be shown off in compotes and cake stands, containers that might be used to hold the real thing.

A sunlit niche helps to capture the earthy properties of a pottery collection in which even shards have a place of honor. Not every object in a collection needs to be perfect.

Crystal candleholders with a variety of bases are lit en masse in front of a mirror, both to illuminate and to decorate a room for an evening of entertaining.

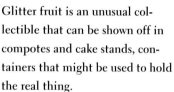

LEFT: When objects are highly colorful and figurative in themselves, such as this collection of ceramics, a simple background—plain but sturdy—helps them stand out. **RIGHT:** A collection of clear crystal finds a suitable home in an elegant corner cabinet that highlights both the glass and the architectural detailing.

Unusual fish trophies, arranged as a circular wall display instead of in regimental rows, show that even the oddest collection can serve a decorative purpose.

Setting out collections museum-style, as in this amateur natural scientist's den, speaks to a passion for imposing logical order on archeological and other finds.

Cherished culinary objects, such as this diverse assortment of copper baking molds, are at their best when brought together in a kitchen setting against a log wall.

LEFT: A recreation room is an appropriate venue for the sport of collecting on the eccentric side, like this billiards room decorated with room keys from around the world. **RIGHT:** Elegant glassware displayed on glass shelves gives interest to a window without a view, at the same time basking to advantage in the natural light.

ABOVE: On simple shelving, a duck and goose decoy collection calls attention to the venerable tradition of wildlife carving. **BELOW:** Black "character dolls," now recognized as genuine folk art, are on display atop an old chest.

ABOVE: Toleware and painted tins and trays are exhibited in a painted cupboard. **BELOW:** It takes only a few outstanding examples of craftsmanship, such as these fine Shaker pantry boxes, to make a forceful decorative statement.

When a favorite animal is the collecting theme, it is fun to mix rare and common expressions of the figure. A cat lover has assembled stuffed, carved, and ceramic models of her favorite pet before a hooked rug with its pair of cats. This kind of menagerie offers limitless possibilities for collectors with a good eye and a sense of humor. Collections based on a theme are often also the easiest to put together—the hard part is knowing when to stop.

The best way to exploit the decorative potential of some collections is by using appropriate containers for them. An old basket holds a jumble of tiny needlepoint pillows, while the rustic cradle is the perfect place to hold a play group of Amish cloth dolls. Collecting child's toys can be a family activity, shared by parents and children alike.

A collection need not be fancy to be worthy of attention. These different-sized and multi-colored bottles fashioned into a see-through wall in Florida are an expression of their owner's talents and playfulness. When a collection such as this is displayed outdoors, of course, the character of the neighborhood must be taken into account.

ABOVE: Folk art, including paintings, a carved wooden head, and a crucifix decorated with bottle caps, is arranged as an altar of whimsy in the home of a collector who values the artifacts of popular culture for their lack of affectation. **BELOW:** A bench and the floor beneath it combine to create exhibit space for a prized collection of Native American baskets and jugs. For large collections, the floor is often the best for displaying but dangerous for valuables. Here the bench provides some protection.

ABOVE: Masks and other mementos of the observance of the Day of the Dead in Mexico are less macabre than might be expected in a room with a wall decorated with vintage automobile hubcaps. **BELOW:** Instead of the usual floral centerpiece, a glass table in the center of the room holds a collection of globes, each more interesting for being part of such a contrasting group.

ABOVE: Family photographs dug out of storage and inexpensively framed allow a wall to be decorated quickly and effectively. The random arrangement of the pictures allows for future additions. **BELOW:** Identically framed botanical prints were hung as a set on a floral-papered wall. The symmetrical arrangement of the pictures helps the viewer to see the botanicals and not the busy background. If the cost is not prohibitive, an entire wall can be filled in this fashion, creating an overall "wallpaper" pattern.

ABOVE: An informal arrangement of pictures and frames shows that images can be as effectively displayed on a tabletop as on a wall. **BELOW:** Fracturs, the illuminated family documents handed down by generations in families of German heritage, are appreciated not only for their antiquity and lineage, but also for their decorative borders, watercolor designs, and hand-lettering. Hearts are featured prominently in the designs, so fracturs also appear in collections centered around that motif.

Foraging in the natural world for objects to decorate the house can produce unexpectedly satisfying results. The outdoor bench of a country retreat has grown into a record of the finds of family and friends on hikes along the river. Not only does a collection of river stones have a strong visual and sensual appeal, it also has the advantage of being easy and inexpensive to acquire—and simple to disperse when it no longer pleases the eye.

A collection of seashells is a decorative display on center stage or in an out-of-the-way nook. Other found objects that can be easily retrieved from nature for makeshift collections include birds' nests, pinecones, fossils, arrowheads, and even beach glass. Since shells have inspired a host of other decorative objects—from rococo furniture to Victorian shellwork boxes—a shell theme collection can feature a range of natural and manmade forms.

Bleached skulls discovered by a walker in the Florida wild are gathered as a tribute to native species, amid shells and other beachcombing detritus. Most other states do not boast alligators (the skull on the far right) as native species, but every geographic region has its own distinctive flora and fauna from which to build a collection that is both decorative and informative.

Antique telescopes sheathed in brass and leather make a handsome display on a mantel or desktop. Tools of the trade, once used in nautical and other professions, show their age and character in a way mass-produced collectibles cannot. And tools are a collectible enjoyed by both men and women, at home in the den, hallway, or living room. Many shops now specialize in small antiques with a masculine theme.

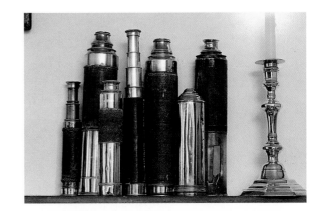

Sometimes the decorative value of an assemblage derives from the dominant material, in this case the wicker covering a tray and its contents of bottles and cups. In colonial India these bottles kept contents cool and provided some protection from breakage. Now they make a handsome portable bar.

Massed together in the line of duty, old watering cans have a surprisingly commanding presence. Overhead racks, hooks, and other devices allow practical implements to be displayed for their esthetic value when not in use. In this case it is the similarity between the collectibles rather than their differences that makes the groupings work so well together.

cup-
boards

Proud fixtures of early American life, cupboards solved the storage problem in houses where closets were conspicuous for their absence. For me, they are the most useful pieces of furniture I own. Armoires, jelly cupboards, Welsh dressers, linen presses, and hutches all offer ample space for storing and displaying housewares, textiles, and other collectibles. The old painted surfaces on cupboards, often decorated and carved, make the plainest pottery look like heirlooms, and the fanciest china feel at home, too. Great in the kitchen, used in place of stock cabinets, these pieces also can function as practical entertainment centers in a living room. Far from detracting from their appeal, nicks and scratches give cupboards a rustic character, perfect for the sophisticated homeowner or active family. In small rooms, they'll fit in awkward corners.  Wherever they are used, cupboards accomplish their traditional humble task of storage, while furnishing a room in style.

PRECEDING PAGES: Cupboards lend character to a room, not only with their myriad shapes and patinaed surfaces, but with the household vessels, dishware, linens, and other collections, often visible from the room, stored within. **LEFT:** A room with no fitted cabinetry depends on old cabinets and cupboards for its decorative style as well as its storage capacity. **ABOVE:** The corner cupboard is an integral part of a room's decoration because it and its contents are visible from all vantage points. **BELOW:** A painted cupboard pleases the eye with its original paint, and serves as a convenient base for a collection of carved birds and crocks.

A plain cupboard has received surface decoration. Sponged, brushed, and stenciled surfaces are common country decoration on nineteenth-century American furniture.

A pine Welsh dresser makes a stately focal point and affords the room a chance to display collections of Majolica pottery and Tennessee baskets.

A small corner cupboard helps to decorate what otherwise might be wasted space. Corner cupboards are often the most sensible designs for today's small interiors.

LEFT: The colorful dishware in the built-in cabinet can be enjoyed whether the glass doors are open or closed. Since it doesn't extend to the floor, the cabinet allows the space beneath it to be used for other purposes. **RIGHT:** A painted and decorated cupboard becomes even more prominent when placed catercorner.

New kitchen cabinets acquire instant vintage with the glass-fronted doors, also a practical touch which saves hunting time for the busy entertainer.

A cupboard with the doors missing can still find a decorative role to play, in this case as an informal bar in a barn that is used for summer entertaining.

A built-in case for a teapot and cups and plates in vertical racks has carved details as elegant as the china pattern it displays.

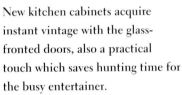

LEFT: An armoire's open-door policy permits its voluminous bed and bath linen collection to be appreciated. **RIGHT:** The top of a faux-grained cupboard is the stopping place for a set of prized but fragile bandboxes. Since this paneled cupboard is most often seen with the doors closed, it can be decorated with a country wreath.

ABOVE: The upper half of an old cupboard in disrepair has been salvaged for use as hanging shelves with a cupboard's function. **BELOW:** An entire wall in this newly built kitchen was given the cupboard treatment, with open shelving above and solid doors below.

ABOVE: Like an old Hoosier cabinet, a well-designed modern kitchen offers a multitude of storage options, ranging from bins to compartments to shelves. **BELOW:** A dark-colored cupboard filled with colorful spongeware creates a decorative tableau.

ABOVE: Fulfilling the functions of old-fashioned cabinets, a new kitchen uses both glass-fronted and solid doors. BELOW: By painting woodwork in a hue related to the original paint of an antique cupboard, a unified scheme has been created for the room.

Cupboards and Cabinets

Although the terms are often used interchangeably, a cupboard refers to case furniture with shelves enclosed by solid doors, whereas a cabinet usually has lots of small drawers and compartments and is often enclosed by glass doors. A cupboard tends to be primitive or rustic, as humble as the one belonging to Mother Hubbard. A cabinet puts on more airs and calls attention to itself as furniture. Both pieces of furniture have a long and checkered history. The cupboard got its name in the Middle Ages because it was used to store and display cups, goblets, and dishes. Armoires, linen presses, and wardrobes are other early variants of the cupboard. The earliest cabinets were products of the Italian Renaissance, used to store and display small objects, but not necessarily kitchenware. Utility was secondary to the exterior appearance of the cabinet, which was often made from exotic woods, or soft woods covered with expensive veneers, and designed with classical architectural motifs. A carpenter or joiner made everyday furnishings, but to this day the term "cabinetmaker" refers to a high order of craftsman.

ABOVE: An elaborately painted and trimmed corner cabinet with Federal period lines makes as assertive a decorative statement in this dining room as the statuary. **BELOW:** This imposing four-door wardrobe is the anchor of a carefully orchestrated grouping.

ABOVE: A dramatic display of animal figures helps to give a built-in storage unit the look of furniture in a sleek kitchen. **BELOW:** Oriental collectibles amassed atop a farm cupboard offer a contrast in both culture and style.

A B O V E : A built-in cupboard in a Southwestern adobe house becomes a window on the world of antique pottery, complete with lace curtains. **B E L O W :** An old spice cupboard has room for a playful collection of figures and toys.

A B O V E : An awkward corner space in a farmhouse has been revitalized by giving the cupboard doors the Picasso treatment. **B E L O W :** Like the fireplace in this grandiose dining room, the cupboard was designed to impress, showcasing pieces of heirloom china.

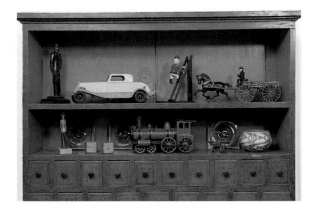

A miscellany of favorite things, including animal and human figures, has been arranged to be appreciated in vignettes through the glass doors of a cupboard.

When a china pattern is sufficiently striking, it can stand on its own as an artistic exhibit, especially in this elegant cabinet with its thin arched mullions.

Everyday bowls, molds, and canisters, bonded in color, occupy a primitive cupboard. Although the doors are not glazed, they can be left open for display.

LEFT: An open cupboard, stacked with linens, quilts, and blankets, fills a room with colors and patterns. **RIGHT:** Old doors were freshly painted with old-fashioned roses, reflecting the artist's passion for gardening. The potted plant beside an antique birdhouse creates a miniature landscape atop this cupboard.

Corner cupboards were very popular in Pennsylvania in the nineteenth century. This twelve-paned cupboard was given a tiger maple finish to make it look fancy.

The surfaces of a stepback cupboard with its original paint and doors contribute as much rustic character to the room as the collection of country pottery.

An unvarnished cupboard offers great storage and a neutral backdrop for the figurative pattern on the blue-and-white Cantonware.

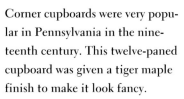

LEFT: Adding an antique furniture scarf takes the rustic edge off an old cupboard, providing a romantic decorative flourish.
RIGHT: An old-fashioned capacious kitchen has the aura of a paneled room thanks to its generous banks of built-in cupboards.

doors

Architects

and builders have always paid special attention to doors, especially front doors, because they so visibly announce the personality of a house to the outside world. If a door has an overly subdued appearance, it can be enlivened by painting it a bright color, exchanging its hardware for something showier, like brass, or introducing a tub of flowers or an eye-catching decorative element, such as a twig heart or ornamental wreath, conveying the message "We're home!" A door can be framed by porch pediments or an arch, emphasizing the entrance. Doors in the interior of the house can serve as a decorative feature when solid wood panels are replaced with etched, leaded, or paned glass. French doors opening onto a porch or patio allow enjoyment of the outside world in every season. Inside and out, doors can be played up or down with techniques such as stenciling, painting, staining, and even papering.

PRECEDING PAGES: Whether on the inside looking out, or on the outside looking in, the door is always one of the most magnetic focal points in a house. **LEFT:** With a decorative personality of their own, Dutch doors infuse a room with a welcoming informality. **ABOVE:** An original expression for a door, this hand-lettered tin carryall offers a festive hello to callers. **BELOW:** Welcome mats and doorstops are decorative accessories that can be used to enhance any portal.

A classic door treatment for an old-fashioned house limits embellishments to basic hardware and the street number.

Adding a trellis to the entranceway, in this case one that echoes the arched transom over the door, is one way to give distinction to a home's facade.

The charming design of an old screen door and abundant carpenter Gothic gingerbread make this inviting porch that much more approachable.

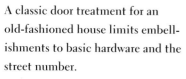

LEFT: The use of contrasting historic paint colors accentuates the architecture of both the paneled door and broken pediment on this Colonial house. **RIGHT:** Paired doors, painted and hung with period wrought-iron hardware, make a notable entrance. The matching curves add grace whether the doors are open or closed.

A pair of wood shutters, still with the old paint job and lunar motif, were recycled to frame a conventional windowed and paneled door with elements of the past.

Dutch doors with an antique leaded-glass transom window offer several ways to bring light into the house.

Symmetrically placed gateposts emphasize the basic geometry of the facade and the five-pane fanlight over the door.

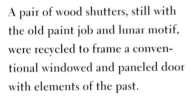

LEFT: Both window and doorframe in this stone house have anthropomorphic eyebrows. The glass door admits light and breaks the somber heaviness of the stone. **RIGHT:** Leafy standards behind slender classical columns on a formal porch imbue a front door with an aura of elegance.

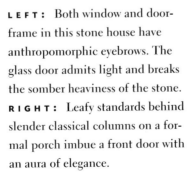

A log house with its front door set within an imposing stone facade gives an impression of grandeur, but reveals its country roots in porch furnishings such as the washtub, the anvil, and a milk can. The strong horizontal and vertical lines of porch steps, posts, beams, and logs are attention-getting features.

Decorative translucent double glass doors enjoy the classic embrace of pillars and urns, as imposing at night, when illuminated, as by day. The candle lantern hanging over the doorway is both an elegant and a practical touch. The sweeping entrance flanked by foundation plantings of ornamental shrubbery leads the eye and the visitor to the door.

The carved decorative molding on the door and surround is echoed by the living foliage that has been trained to frame the entrance in green throughout the year. A rectangular transom and sidelights let light into the entryway and allow the homeowner to observe visitors before admitting them.

Leaded glass doors add panels of art to a house, at the same time providing privacy where needed. Unlike solid doors, these doors preserve an open feeling in a floor plan even when they are closed. When introduced into a new house, they should be used sparingly for effect so as not to dilute their impact.

Two pairs of full-width French doors allow generous access to a screened porch, as well as enjoyment of the light and atmosphere of the porch whether the doors are opened or closed. As handsome architectural features, they are an excellent alternative to the standard sliding doors so often found between the house and the porch or patio.

A pair of old doors receive a refreshing new look with panels of glass sand-blasted in pleasing graphic designs. Such doors can be enjoyed as architectural elements in their own right, especially when flanked by other strong elements, such as the two columns here. The placement of the mirror echoes the position of the glass in the doors.

The Front Door in Four Seasons

More than any other single element in the house, the front door lends itself to seasonal decoration. Often, the materials naturally at hand at different times of the year can be adapted for this purpose. In early spring, rustic containers filled with pansies or primroses help the front entrance get a jump on the season. Summer is a good time to take advantage of a sunny front door with standards of roses, rosemary, or lavender. Or plant up a favorite container with the colorful annuals that do well in your area. The front door of a summer house at the shore might celebrate its regional character with wind chimes fashioned from seashells or driftwood. In the fall, there are pumpkins, Indian corn, and gourds to set the theme, and all manner of wreaths and bunches fashioned from freshly harvested and dried flowers and herbs. Come winter, with the house made ready for the holidays, the front door might take on a festive character, with a display of antique sleigh bells, elegant boxwood roping, or a wreath made of pinecones, holly, or bright red chili peppers.

ABOVE: The front door needs furnishing too. Here, genteel finishing touches include an antique umbrella stand and a brightly patterned throw rug. **BELOW:** A series of Dutch doors off a courtyard plays gray against pink.

An exterior door made of metal grillwork, designed primarily for security reasons, offers itself as a visual treat when the interior door is left ajar.

When the view is spectacular, a house's screen door, like this light wooden one, should be as unobtrusive as possible.

Working in harmony with a black-and-white tiled floor, a sophisticated custom door design turns a claustrophic hallway into an inviting vestibule.

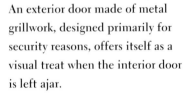

LEFT: A double door built into the solid wall supporting a sweeping staircase offers stylish passage through an arch into an important room. **RIGHT:** An adobe house in the Southwest glories in a heavy carved Spanish Colonial door, which opens onto the interior courtyard that is the hallmark of Spanish architecture.

dressers, dressing tables & mirrors

Some furnishings appeal to our sense of vanity—our need to look our best and to know what we look like as we come and go. Mirrors allow our changing images to join the rest of the home's decor. In the bedroom, the mirror can create romance. The old-fashioned vanity table, where women pampered themselves with powders and fragrances and pots of rouge, retains a sentimental hold on the imagination today. Here small collectibles add their romantic note to the decor. A china bowl is used for potpourri, a favorite platter holds jewelry, silver-topped bottles and jars contain cosmetic supplies, and tiny silver picture frames remind us of familiar faces. No vanity is complete without at least one mirror, and the more the merrier. A collection of hand mirrors makes a stunning wall arrangement, for example. Depending on the frame, mirrors can be witty, dramatic, classical, or baroque. No matter what style, a strategically placed mirror can make a room look larger and serve as a glittering focal point.

PRECEDING PAGES: Mirrors are the one indispensable element in every vanity. An ornate gilt mirror is the perfect match for a commode adapted for use as a dressing table, while hand mirrors, arranged on the wall in a group, complement an antique china pitcher and washbowl. LEFT: Three convex mirrors of differing origins are brought together in a dressing room where Victoriana reigns supreme. ABOVE: A framed mirror with fan detail was selected to give height and importance to an antique dresser. The candlestick lamps and pair of chairs complete the grouping. BELOW: Even a small mirror that wears its age gracefully can transform a bathroom corner.

ABOVE: A vanity has been improvised with a small table placed in the middle of the bathing area, fully equipped for a lady's toilette. **BELOW:** A horned cup, silver-topped bottles, and tortoiseshell-lidded jars keep beauty supplies at hand on the dressing table.

ABOVE: A bedroom vanity consists of a marble-topped chest of drawers with two antique mirrors. **BELOW:** A small lamp lends atmosphere to the top of a dresser where baskets, glass bottles, and a silver-handled dresser set provide the sheen and sparkle.

ABOVE: The addition of a freestanding mirror allows a beautiful antique chest with faux-grained surfaces to serve as a dresser. **BELOW:** A rustic cupboard becomes an elegant dressing table when decorated with a punched-tin mirror and dried topiaries.

ABOVE: Appropriated as a dresser, the early American blanket chest holds a miniature chest, used to store jewelry, and chair. Instead of a mirror, a primitive portrait looks over the room. **BELOW:** A drop-leaf table with drawers functions as a vanity.

An old picture frame, revived with new mirror glass and embraced by a galaxy of straw hats, is the centerpiece of a bedroom dresser used as a vanity.

The frame for the mirror was painted to coordinate with the console table and the carved wreath—a formal look accentuated by candlestick lamps.

A plain cottage cupboard paired with a gilt-framed mirror enlivens a simple landing and reflects the light from the window into the stairwell.

LEFT: A faux bamboo mirror frame and dresser make an enticing service bar in the living room with the addition of a silver tray and candlestick lamps. RIGHT: Whether an entry hall is grand or apartment-size, the presence of a stately mirror helps to welcome visitors, who can check their appearance before joining the party.

A junk shop mirror is the finishing touch in a summer house bathroom with a nautical feeling, from the caged lighting to the striped skirt on the sink.

With its frame painted white to blend with the wall and dresser, this oval mirror unobtrusively expands the room.

The wood mirror in this W.C., with its own sconces and an exaggerated pediment, focuses attention on the simple sink with towel bar below.

LEFT: The ornate girandole mirror, its convex glass reflecting the world as the eagle might see it, is most at home in a formal setting.
RIGHT: An oversize mirror fills a narrow room with light and reflection, visually expanding space where it is at a premium. Its height allows even the chandelier to be reflected.

ABOVE: A baroque mirror was the inspiration for a hall treatment that carries decoration to a playful extreme. **BELOW:** A shell collection makes twice the impact when arranged in front of a mirror, placed horizontally to match the length of the mantel.

ABOVE: The arched mirror over a console table extends its reach with a witty homemade twig trophy. **BELOW:** This venerable overmantel mirror with pediment, curves, and fluted panels is used as a piece of sculpture leaning against the wall.

ABOVE: An ornately carved stone fireplace called for a mirror with the same elegant scale and flourishes in this setting of benign decadence. **BELOW:** A gilt mirror crowned with its own laurel garland sets off a pair of octagonal picture frames.

ABOVE: Successfully mixing the sublime with the ridiculous, this room combines a mirror from the age of Napoleon with a specimen of roadside Americana. **BELOW:** Mirrors collected at random make a happy composition when combined with a draped banner.

flowers

Like many people, I am happiest in the summertime, when I can enjoy the beach, the warm breezes, and the pleasures of the garden. Whatever the season, I have to have flowers—cut or potted—indoors. Flowers bring such color, warmth, gaiety, and romance to the home, at such modest expense and effort, that they are the most flexible and useful decorative element. Anything from a fine crystal bud vase to a humble old milk bottle can be used to hold flowers. The secret is to match the blooms to the container, taking into consideration the character of the flowers and the shape, texture, and color of the vessel, and then to place the creation in the setting it deserves. The process is more art than science: the eye is the best guide to making a bouquet, but there are many books available that give advice on conditioning, selecting, and arranging flowers. The most useful tip is not to be afraid of mistakes. Decorating a room with flowers is a pleasure in the doing, and the result is a joyful presence that can linger for days.

PRECEDING PAGES: Flowers and the containers they are displayed in can be as elegant as roses floating in English porcelain or as informal as country blooms gathered in old milk bottles. **LEFT:** Banks of geraniums in identical terra-cotta pots, showing there is strength in numbers, make a powerful backdrop for a breakfast table. **ABOVE:** A bouquet of paper ranunculas in a timeworn urn adds color to a collection of ancient carvings. **BELOW:** Summer flowers have been cut on the short side so that the woven basket appears filled to the brim with blooms.

A crock taken down from the cupboard serves as a vase for an informal gathering of cut flowers in a still life of collectibles.

Tools of farm and garden, such as pails and watering cans, are well suited for country bouquets on porches, picnic tables, and even a stepstool pedestal.

A monochromatic display of Queen Anne's lace in a painted bucket makes a striking centerpiece when teamed with simple candles.

LEFT: A cutting from the French lilac bush in the spring effortlessly lends beauty and fragrance to a work station.
RIGHT: This perky arrangement has been set out in a rustic pot, a container that doesn't compete with the flowers for attention.

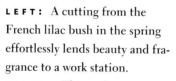

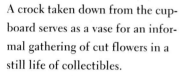

A milk pitcher filled with field cuttings is an unexpected presence on a sunny window ledge.

A palate of weathered colors dictated this arrangement of flowers and furnishings.

The pedestal table departs from tradition, holding untamed coreopsis in a country crock.

LEFT: An arrangement of roses and baby's breath, with trailing vines, completes the romantic dress-whites look of the table.
RIGHT: A mass of dried flowers, all in pale hues and packed head to head in a low basket, makes an impressive everlasting bouquet that adorns the coffee table without intruding on conversation.

ABOVE: Collections of small bottles and other containers can be adapted for a single-file display of individual blossoms. **BELOW:** Identical vases from the 1920s are used to make a matched set of sunflowers and <u>Q</u>ueen Anne's lace.

ABOVE: Tropical flowers are a suitably voluptuous accompaniment for exotic art and sculpture.
BELOW: A graduated collection of lively polka dot ceramics holds a bunch of dahlias from the garden.

ABOVE: A glamorous tabletop setting invites a flower treatment that emphasizes the elegant rather than the plain, in this case, white peonies in a crystal vase. **BELOW:** A richly textured wreath, studded with dried roses, makes an attractive wall display.

ABOVE: A shapely goblet vase is well suited for a delicate bouquet of lilies and lilacs, designed to complement the Victorian setting. Two old condiment containers serve as vases for the roses. **BELOW:** Wildflowers gathered along the roadside fill a room.

ABOVE: Suitable props for flowers range far beyond the standard florist shop containers, just as the flowers themselves can come from more places than one. Here, cotton bolls harvested with stems intact make a surprisingly vivid display in an old toy wagon made from scrap wood. BELOW: The old wire bottle carrier is called back into service as a flower stand, large and charming enough to be a table decoration.

ABOVE: Climbing roses in an elegant painted vase become part of an artful still life composition on a log cabin wall. BELOW: Dried hydrangeas in an English ironstone bucket combine with painted pansies to infuse a room with lasting beauty. Dried flowers extend the pleasure of gardening throughout the year, and can be combined with branches, grasses, and dried herbs for volume and effect.

ABOVE: Sunflowers are becoming increasingly popular. With their reference to the paintings of van Gogh they almost seem like art come to life. Here they become twice as showy when placed in front of a mirror. **BELOW:** Pots of geraniums, one of the most reliable flowers indoors or out, have been organized on an old footed tray. Not only does the tray protect the floor from water damage, it also helps make a bold decorative statement.

ABOVE: An English china teapot is used to show off a fresh bouquet of roses. Teapots that have lost their tops are often relegated to the tag sale table and can be collected by the prudent shopper to be used as flower vases. **BELOW:** Nothing is more romantic or fragrant than a summer rose at the height of bloom. Here arranged in a low modest container to act as a centerpiece, these pale pink roses are a vision of the generosity of the garden beyond.

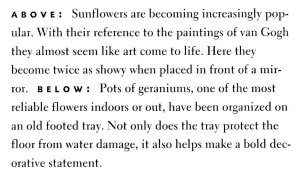

garden

elements

Gardens are outdoor rooms. Once that is understood, it is possible to consider a wide range of furnishings and other objects to decorate them with. Not only do these elements help to define and enhance the garden, they often can be useful in their own right, such as a trellis for training climbing vines, a chair providing the gardener a chance to catch her breath, or a scarecrow giving birds second thoughts about invading the berry patch. Whimsical signs and folk art ornaments help to humanize any garden that doesn't necessarily aspire to be a botanical masterpiece. Stepping stones invite visitors into the garden. More ambitiously, a pavilion or a gazebo provides a shady place to share lemonade with friends and also  enjoy the garden at close range. The more the garden offers seats for reading and contemplation, tables for dining, and chaise longues for naps, the more likely it is that friends and family will enjoy the effort it took to make it beautiful.

PRECEDING PAGES: The features that help to show off the plants in a garden may be as pronounced as a traditional picket fence complete with arbors or as subtle as a shapely painted pot. **LEFT:** A log pavilion lures visitors to the garden, adding a striking architectural element to the landscape and offering protection from the sun. **ABOVE:** A floor-to-ceiling trellis gives the gardener the luxury of training any number of climbing vines to bedeck the house with foliage and flowers. **BELOW:** The workhorse of any garden, the wheelbarrow also contributes aesthetic appeal when it is stamped with time.

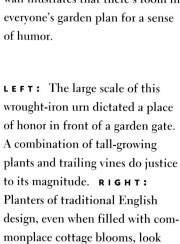

Even when gardening space is unlimited, containers like this one bursting with dianthus and lobelia add interest, style, and fragrance at close range to the garden scene.

A folk art fish on a painted white wall illustrates that there's room in everyone's garden plan for a sense of humor.

A classic white garden urn contains plants that commensurate with its stately bearing.

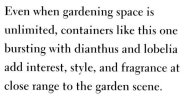

LEFT: The large scale of this wrought-iron urn dictated a place of honor in front of a garden gate. A combination of tall-growing plants and trailing vines do justice to its magnitude. **RIGHT:** Planters of traditional English design, even when filled with commonplace cottage blooms, look their best in traditional settings.

A gracefully arched trellis with an echoing garden gate provides a romantic welcome to the garden and a frame for the cottage.

This painted trellis, handcrafted with a bird motif, makes an effective backdrop for the perennial border. A trellis is a graphic statement as well as a practical support.

Architectural relics fully integrated into the garden plan can delight the eye as sculpture and offer a point of contrast to the natural palette of green.

LEFT: More decorative than a plain planter, this cast stone pot lends its Italian fruit and garlands decoration to a gardenside terrace. **RIGHT:** The giant escargot helps give definition to an herb garden, where the small scale of the delicate plants benefits from contrasting forms.

ABOVE: Folk art is as much at home in the garden as a rooster in the henhouse. **BELOW:** Potted flowers can be used to perk up out-of-the-way perches. In the summer, rotate potted plants in and out of the garden as they come into bloom.

ABOVE: A universal figure in country gardens, the scarecrow can be gotten up in just about any outfit. **BELOW:** Adding one or more walls to a garden defines the perimeter of the growing area and provides a decorative background for plantings.

ABOVE: A busy barn wall and walkways made of brick help to set off an herb garden in rustic style.
BELOW: A shingle-roof dovecote is an eye-catching vertical element in a perennial border. Local garden tours will yield a bounty of good ideas.

ABOVE: A garden of specimen shrubs and bushes is marked by a manicured lawn and centered by a carved stone pedestal. **BELOW:** Any arrangement of planted pots of many sizes on a porch or deck creates an agreeable patch of garden color.

ABOVE: In expansive gardens, tall architectural structures such as this wooden obelisk often contribute a much-needed vertical dimension. **BELOW:** A tall hedge, an old stone wall, and traditional seating enclose and furnish an open-air room.

ABOVE: Garden furniture need not be limited to pieces designed expressly for outdoor use. This ice cream parlor chair survives wet weather with an extra coat of paint. **BELOW:** Grouping flowering plants in containers allows for portability.

Rustic outdoor furnishings like this twig armchair, which only improves in looks as it ages and weathers, are the natural inhabitants of a country garden.

Birdhouses are increasingly popular as gardeners try to attract birds for their insect-control potential, and collectors increasingly appreciate their appeal as folk art.

An Italianate container is planted with a medley of flora. Containers can be replanted in the course of the season to dress the garden in different colors.

LEFT: A painted bench turns a tiny grove of trees into an irresistible destination for visitors to the garden. **RIGHT:** A rustic screened structure with its stag weathervane serves as a dining pavilion on a large property. It offers the intimacy of a small room in tandem with the openness of the outdoors.

The painted wood gate stands out brightly in the middle of a tumbledown stone wall, naturally leading the eye to the house in the distance. Although stone walls once rose easily in rural areas as farmers cleared their land for cultivation, they can now be costly to install and should be cherished where they already exist.

Discards from the woodlot were salvaged to build a unique log wall to separate the vegetable garden from the flowering meadow. In addition to this practical function, a fence can "decorate" the outdoor or divide open spaces.

Fencing can be made of a wide variety of materials. The more confined the garden, the more important the look of the fence becomes. Fences and walls are complementary backgrounds for flowering plants. Lilies and perennials in wild profusion are at home in front of this traditional white picket fence with its orderly and upright personality. It may deter a few garden invaders, but a picket fence primarily serves as a boundary marker and decorative element.

As a viewing platform for admiring the garden, and a spare room in the outdoors, the back porch, when furnished with comfortable seating, is the best place to put up your feet after a session of weeding and watering. Since so much time is spent here from spring to fall, the painting of wall, floor, and trim should be carefully considered.

Flowering shrubs revisit the garden every year at about the same time, adding their beauty with little effort on the gardener's part and bringing along their spirit of renewal. They are the preferred alternative to conventional foundation plantings, especially in a country house. Here rhododendrons make a spectacle at the corner of a shingled house.

A simple painted bench that once made its home in a one-room schoolhouse or on the porch of a country store adds an accent of color and design, at the same time providing another vantage point from which the visitor can view the garden scene.

lamps

&

candles

Interior

lighting can be soft, soothing, intimate, and flattering, especially when the source is candles, decorative table lamps, or wall sconces. Used strategically, these small lighting features can all but replace overhead lighting systems that tend to remove mood and atmosphere from a room. The art of decorating with light is really the challenge of finding the right combination of small-scale illumination for the particular room and, when a romantic occasion demands, supplementing that with lots of candles—preferably of the nonscented kind. Since electric lighting came into general use only in our century, there are few legitimate antique lamps, but charming one-of-a-kind lamps can be created from crocks, tea tins, urns, statuary, baskets, and many other objets trouvés. Because they suit both indoor and outdoor settings, glass hurricane shades are one of the best ways to display candles, but the many other varieties of candles and candlesticks available provide an endless array of possibilities.

PRECEDING PAGES: Soft light, whether it is cast by a unique lantern in the shape of a pineapple or pillars of candle wax, establishes a mood no other kind of lighting can achieve. **LEFT:** An ocean of votive lights on silver pedestals creates an unforgettable table centerpiece. **ABOVE:** A pair of handcrafted metal candleholders can be appreciated for their own beauty as well as their practical use. **BELOW:** Dressed up with a plaid shade, a little brown jug enjoys new life as a decorative table lamp in a cottage setting.

Two examples of far-out folk art, a hand-punched tin shade and a base covered with native stone, give this lamp a rustic personality.

A lamp performs double duty when its transparent base is used to show off a beachcomber's treasures, which take on an intense glow under the light.

In a traditional bedroom, a lamp base of urn and candlestick is topped with an elegant black shade with gold trim.

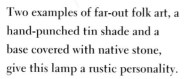

LEFT: Retrieved from the pantry, an old yellow crock lamp now serves admirably on a skirted table in the bedroom. A very simple shade gives the crock a feeling of dignity; a more fanciful shade might make it seem more amusing. **RIGHT:** A custom-made silk shade befitting an emperor crowns a Chinese porcelain base.

ABOVE: An art collection receives discreet illumination from an artfully shaped paper lantern. **BELOW:** An outdoor light fixture was added to this guard-dog gargoyle to help with street security.

ABOVE: A curvaceous corner interior receives its decorative coup de grâce with a sculpted solid brass lamp. **BELOW:** A humble barrel-base lamp comes up in the world with a stitched cowhide shade.

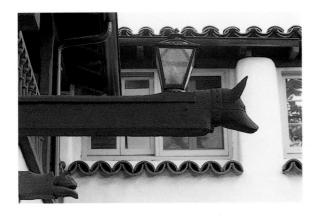

ABOVE: Lamps are an extension of a room's personality. In this understated room, the reading light is provided by a handwrought floor lamp with a tailored shade. **BELOW:** Candlesticks on a stone mantel create an aura of romance.

ABOVE: A tiny lamp made from a candlestick serves as a footlight for precious keepsakes and antique images. **BELOW:** In an eclectically furnished camp-style retreat, all lamps are welcome, including an antique metal one with a glass shade.

ABOVE: Lampshades need not be round. This rectangular shape enlivens a plain base. **BELOW:** Found tortoise shells make dramatic wall sconces in a bedroom near the ocean. The reading lamp on the table was created from an old basket.

Decorative Table Lamps

As an alternative to buying lamps in a store, consider making your own, by combining bases originally made for another purpose with standard-issue shades. Wiring can be inexpensively supplied by a local repair shop, or do-it-yourself kits are available in stores or by mail order. Just about any container can be turned into a lamp base. Painted tea canisters, stoneware jugs, Staffordshire figures, wooden candlesticks, urns, vases, and even loving cup trophies all can serve as winning lamp bases when paired with the appropriate shade. (If it's a treasured antique, though, bear in mind that the alteration will reduce the value of the piece.) A base made from a clear glass jar can be filled with seashells, glass marbles, pinecones, smooth pebbles, or other eye-catching materials. The shade itself can be wrapped with fabric or wallpaper, découpaged with favorite pictures, or hand-painted with a pretty design. Decorative trim like braid and fringe can be added to the shade to make it fancier. By fashioning your own table lamps, you can light up any room with a custom look.

An etched glass hurricane lamp needs only a prominent place and the light of one candle to share its fragile beauty with the room.

In a farmhouse setting, an antique kerosene wall fixture has a glass hurricane shade as well as a built-in fireguard.

A handmade wrought-iron wall sconce sheds light on art representing the culture and geography of the Southwest.

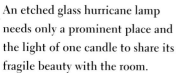

LEFT: The candlestick is part of a carefully arranged still life on a hammered metal shelf. **RIGHT:** An elegant framed mirror gives depth to a tabletop composition by reflecting the light of the tapers, in brass candlesticks of different design.

Mounted on its own wrought-iron stand, the oversize glass candleholder, lined with decorative moss, provides a pretty way to light a terrace or porch at night.

A richly carved and detailed candelabrum adds a touch of splendor to an empty wall, while the actual light comes from the diminutive lamp below.

With the addition of a candle, an oversized handblown glass goblet serves as a useful and attractive hurricane lamp.

LEFT: The elegant ginger jar table lamp makes an agreeable bedside companion to the blue and white table quilt. **RIGHT:** A table with simple but enduring lines finds its match in a lamp made from a pleasantly plump stoneware pot and capped with a classic shade.

mantels

The fireplace mantel is a natural focal point in a room, a display area, located at eye level, for prized possessions and favorite collectibles. It is so prominent, in fact, that I change the tableaux on my mantels frequently, to keep the look fresh and appealing. Mantels with distinctive architectural or period lineage invite decorative treatments that evoke the same style. A rustic Colonial hearth might be topped with an ancient musket or a collection of primitive birdhouses. The formal mantel of a Georgian house would look at its best with an elegant gilt-edged mirror, for instance, or a matching pair of classic urns. Even the most nondescript mantel can be personalized with the addition of family portraits, a collection that represents someone's sporting passion,  such as bird carvings, or an assemblage of folk art with a single theme. Take the time to decorate a mantel thoughtfully, and you will be rewarded every time you look at it.

PRECEDING PAGES: A fireplace devoted to religious folk art contrasts sharply with the sleek, sophisticated look of a 1930s-style interior, showing the rich and varied opportunities for decoration in mantel treatments. LEFT: An early Colonial hearth is capped with a painted wood mantel and surrounded with tools and ornaments reminiscent of the same era. ABOVE: Trimmed with a birchbark panel, the fireplace mantel in this lodge dwelling evokes its wilderness setting. BELOW: This mantel, painted the same color as the wall, blends into the surroundings, focusing attention on a collection of primitive art.

ABOVE: An unusual antique mirror with built-in candle sconces acts as an overmantel for an old formal fireplace partially stripped of its original paint for effect. **BELOW:** A mantel is an ideal exhibition area for this array of Colonial pewter.

ABOVE: Corner fireplaces in adobe homes often have built-in ledges that are ideal for staging pictures and objects in pleasing displays. **BELOW:** In this symmetrical arrangement, the vertical mantel clock is the apex of a nest of taxidermy creations.

ABOVE: The mantel, chair rail, and molding in this room have been painted to contrast with the walls, calling attention to the traditional architectural detail. **BELOW:** An elaborate overmantel treatment combines mosaic tile art and carved wood.

ABOVE: Many fireplaces allow for display both above and below the mantel. **BELOW:** The carved features of the fireplace in this Southwestern living room have been painted in the spirit of the Native American artifacts on show.

A tall mirror has been playfully turned on its side to act as a backdrop for a collection of framed pictures. The antic quality in the collection of images on top of the mantel provides an amusing counterpoint to the room's authentic furnishings.

The motif of carved waterfowl and shorebird decoys present throughout the room is acknowledged atop the narrow mantel. The painted panel between mantel and hearth adds color to the fireplace without spoiling its character. Painted woodwork throughout the room emphasizes its symmetry.

A fireplace in a room that once functioned as a full-time kitchen is decorated with period cooking utensils and the rifle that at one time brought home the bacon. The mantel has been appropriated for a display of colorful cuttings as a token of the season. Because the fireplace is especially wide it cannot help but be the focus for the room, and the humble furnishings acknowledge its prominence.

Sometimes the wall over the mantel can simply be designed and painted as a decorative element on its own. Here, the display on top of the mantel has been carefully coordinated to complement and not intrude on an original wall painting, which has the impact of trompe l'oeil.

This small Victorian fireplace has been given an importance beyond its size with a riot of primary colors. The hearth still has its original coal grate from the time when coal was used for heating. Although it is not as elaborate as some nineteenth-century mantelpieces, this example has pleasing lines and decorative detailing that deserve to be noticed.

Pewter steins and candleholders with glass chimneys are a subdued presence on the narrow mantel of a Colonial fireplace kept in its original state. Behind the little door on the left of the hearth is the brick oven, where bread was baked. The door over the hearth opens onto the "parson's cupboard," where a bottle of rum might have been kept for the clergyman's visit.

Restoring the Mantel

An unappealing painted mantel can be given a new look by stripping off the old paint and refinishing the surface. Making sure that the room is well ventilated, and wearing rubber gloves, first use a brush to apply paint-stripping gel to the old surface. Use a high-quality product; it's worth it if the mantel is the only stripping project. Leave the gel on the surface for thirty minutes, or the time stipulated in the manufacturer's directions. Once the paint layers have bubbled, scrape off the loosened paint with a putty knife or metal scraper. Repeat the process a second or third time, if necessary, to reach the original bare wood. Then clean the surface using rubbing alcohol. After the wood has dried, use sandpaper and steel wool to smooth the entire surface of the mantel. Wipe the surface clean after sanding. If the mantel is to be left unfinished, a moisturizing agent such as tung oil should be applied to the entire surface. If the mantel is to be painted or stained, seal it first with a coating of furniture varnish. When finished, choose accessories with care; the mantel will now draw attention to its decor.

ABOVE: A bedroom fireplace no longer in commission still makes a grand centerpiece. Note the unusual candlestands that flank the mantel. **BELOW:** When the fireplace is the room's principal visual interest, it is often best to keep decoration to a minimum.

ABOVE: An elaborate carved mantel is a fitting place for showing off elegant paraphernalia.
BELOW: A tiled surround, practical because it shields the edges of the hearth from heat and soot, also makes a bold graphic addition to a stylish interior.

ABOVE: In a playful facelift, a nineteeth-century mantel is adorned with a host of painted stars.
BELOW: In a child's attic bedroom, the fireplace is the garrison for toy soldiers and other favorite dolls.

racks & shelves

Things of utilitarian value are very often beautiful, and I see no reason to hide them away. Left in the open, the objects we need can be easily found; objects we love can be constantly admired. Peg racks, pot racks, plate racks, shelves, built-ins, and wall-hung open cabinets, even recycled wooden rake heads and old stepladders, all can provide pleasing solutions for finding a place for the tools of daily living that elude organization, and for those special things that deserve prominence in a room. Racks and shelves help to make every inch of wall space work for us, not against us. They take advantage of quirky areas such as the flat surface atop an old-fashioned radiator or cupboard, as well as the no-man's-land often found on walls just below the ceiling. In addition to stretching a room's available space, racks and shelves add their own architectural charm. Eye-pleasing workhorses, racks and shelves can earn their keep in any room of the house.

PRECEDING PAGES: For storing cooking utensils or displaying favorite collections, racks and shelves offer versatile solutions for expanding space decoratively. LEFT: A kitchen where the philosophy of open storage is practiced throughout allows the cook access to an impressive array of tools. ABOVE: An old roadside stand fixture, once used to sell fresh fruits and vegetables, now is used to exhibit a watering can collection. BELOW: The small shelf with its carved scalloped profile and painted surface is an eye-catching rustic perch for a collection of antique dolls.

Custom-built open shelves take the place of a china cupboard in this modern kitchen. A spacious counter can be used as a buffet when entertaining or to exhibit an array of serving vessels and favorite objects. Items such as a creamware compote filled with green apples and a pair of candlesticks have been arranged in the most prominent shelf unit to add a decorative note to the service area.

A kitchen with a white-on-white color scheme features an open storage system with a built-in rack for wine-glasses as well as a niche for coffee mugs that creates a welcome change of scale. The constant of same color/similar size can be applied to other kitchen collections by matching wall paint and arranging objects carefully. Neatness counts in such a display, so this may not be the best storage solution for frantic cooks.

The old-fashioned wallpaper pattern can still be appreciated in a kitchen that uses adjustable wire racks, including a shelf suspended from the ceiling, for storing essential items. The dead space over doors and windows should be remembered when planning open storage, as well as the over-counter areas that store items in constant use.

Old racks once used for hats, coats, luggage, or other purposes can be adapted for use in the kitchen as practical organizers with the addition of movable hooks. Almost any kitchen implement can be hung on the wall, readily accessible for the busy cook.

Vertical racks and an overhead shelf making use of the versatile S hook manage to contain everything a busy cook requires within easy reach. Note that pots and pans are hung in series, making maximum use of the wall space and creating the orderly look so important when open storage is the rule. Pot lids are hung above their pots so that they are never missing when the recipe advises to "cover."

In this country kitchen, permanent open shelves were built above the countertop as an alternative to a bank of solid cabinets, to avoid an institutional fitted look. Shelving with handcrafted detailing elicits the same response as a good piece of furniture. Items too unruly for display are stowed away in under-counter cabinets with solid doors.

A recess for shelves, created above an old wood-burning cookstove and used to hold a collection of enameled canisters, makes a spectacular focal point in this kitchen.

In the pantry, the one room seen usually only by the cook, deep and plentiful open shelving is always convenient, whether the clutter is organized or not.

Borrowing the ideas for displaying merchandise used in an old general store, this open-shelf kitchen brims over with a variety of colorful images and receptacles.

LEFT: Peg racks, whether antique Shaker or do-it-yourself, are among the most useful of all room accessories. **RIGHT:** An old country chest serves as a combination bar/pot rack in the dining room.

Built-in bookshelves painted a strong background color have been adapted for a set of antique china.

A simple painted wooden shelf, with brackets mounted on a backboard, adds its mustard hue to a log house's family of old colors.

The shelves in a flamboyantly painted arched recess exhibit a collection of Mexican folk art.

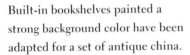

LEFT: Stenciling adds a decorative finish to built-in bookshelves that frame a doorway. **RIGHT:** A diminutive bracketed shelf turns an empty wall space into an arresting niche when paired with an antique instead of smaller, less eye-catching objects.

ABOVE: A peg rack in the bathroom provides two ingenious ways to store fresh towels. **BELOW:** A hard-to-use area under the eaves has been outfitted with storage shelves adorned with shirred fabric and lace trim to make a linen closet.

ABOVE: An antique peg rack installed on modern tile makes a decorative contrast in this open-stall shower. **BELOW:** Wire shelving solves the storage needs of an attic bedroom short on space and, with the use of a few collectibles, also makes a visual statement.

Wicker baskets are an affordable and attractive way to bring order and tidiness to open shelving.

A closet has been retrofitted with shelves and a vintage towel rack to both house and display precious linens and lace.

When the wardrobe consists of colorful vestments, a peg rack adds a lively graphic note to the room and saves time for a family on the go.

LEFT: The addition of a shelf above the bathroom sink provides room for a compact vanity, made attractive with a collection of glasses as containers. **RIGHT:** A pine wall shelf expands its service when wrought-iron nails, some with decorative heads, are used as pegs to hold an abundance of beadwork necklaces.

ABOVE: Shelving need not be at arm's length if the objects are meant to be admired and not used. The dead space near the ceiling in a room is an ideal location for decorative shelving, here used to parade a collection of miniature rustic buildings. **BELOW:** A shelf prized for its color and curves is a winning backdrop for a collection of folk pieces, including two risqué candlesticks.

ABOVE: A sled the size of a toboggan, suspended by chains from the ceiling, is a surprising aerial shelf for other collectibles in a room open to the rafters.

BELOW: The top of a painted cupboard has been used to shelve paint supplies and a variety of books, some with decorative bindings.

An old fold-down ironing board has been converted to a display rack for antique linens.

A knickknack shelf constructed from empty thread spools, relics of the old textile mills, has room for birds of all feathers.

Bunches of dried herbs and flowers are hung from an antique sorting rack adapted for a new purpose and suspended overhead.

LEFT: Recessed shelves help to define miniature figures, making them easier to appreciate.

RIGHT: The decorative impact in this collector's haven comes from the wall of shelves lined with books and the railing used as a hanging rack. For the homeowner who loves a library, bookshelves can be used almost like wallpaper.

tables,
benches
& desks

When I think of tables, benches, and desks, I think of home work—food preparation in the kitchen, carpentry tasks in the workshop, and schoolwork in the study. More than any other kind of furniture, these pieces show the evidence of hand-work, which gives them a nostalgic charm. Then there is their individuality. Apart from having in common a flat surface, tables, benches, and desks can have a wide range of variation in size, style, material, color, and use. Some benches make use-ful tables, and some tables make convenient desks. Often a bench or table with a lackluster surface will come to life with a creative paint job, but some surfaces are best left unaltered, such as the rustic patina on an old workbench, or the polished finish on an antique secretary. And with just a little imagination, favorite tables, benches, and desks can go to work in new guises in the house, on the porch, and even in the garden, playing unaccustomed roles just about anywhere with style and purpose.

PRECEDING PAGES: Common furniture can be used for a variety of purposes, such as a settee offering a cozy place to linger with the addition of cushions, pillows, and footstool, or when a kitchen set is spruced up with a kaleidoscope of fresh colors. **LEFT:** A farm table looks decorated enough to forgo tablecloth or place mats. When it is surrounded by a set of chairs and a long bench, the stage is set for a comfortable informal lunch. **ABOVE:** An old pedestal table was given a new life when its surface was découpaged from head to toe. **BELOW:** A nineteenth-century writing desk of exotic design makes a definite statement in any room. A secret side drawer becomes a ledge for a witty display of fresh flowers.

ABOVE: A Victorian table takes on a new look with a coat of white paint and shawl-draped dining chairs. **BELOW:** An old worktable serves as a versatile coffee table in a colorful country setting.

ABOVE: A handcrafted console table greets visitors with a seasonal tableau. **BELOW:** Clear plate glass can be combined with a surprising number of unusual bases, such as this log dollhouse, to make coffee, side, end, and dining tables.

ABOVE: When a plain twig table is dressed up with a fancy fringed scarf, it can fit in with more elaborate furnishings. BELOW: Set in a romantic garret beneath a draped skylight, a trestle table provides ample surface for spreading out paperwork.

ABOVE: A pine kitchen table, a monumental presence in the room, can handle as many as ten for dinner. The side drawer is handy for cutlery. BELOW: The old painted surface on this harvest table would be lost to view if it was covered with linens.

Natural tripods, harvested in the woods, have been converted into a pair of jaunty rustic tables with matching rectangular wood tops.

The carved bear, a familiar icon in camp furniture of the Victorian era, would originally have been used in a rustic setting.

Two miniature benches, once used as furniture samples and now examples of folk art, are part of the arrangement of an old table set against a wall for display.

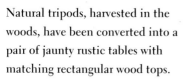

LEFT: A graceful old arched stretcher base was fitted with a stone top to make a stunning library table. **RIGHT:** The combination of table, chair, and lamp, all products of the Arts and Crafts era, creates a useful and aesthetically pleasing desk set.

Like corner cupboards, a corner table fills an otherwise unused space. Here, a European antique holds objects with a bizarre twist, including a folk art armadillo.

An old round butcher's block has a new life as a table.

An old utility table serves unpretentiously in a kitchen of today, its shiny metal surface as decorative as it is practical.

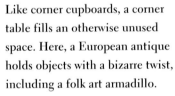

LEFT: A Biedermeier side table was used to anchor an exceptional collection of antiquities in a hall. **RIGHT:** An old side table that owes its beauty to its simple lines and worn surfaces forms the central fixture in this hall display of early American arts and crafts.

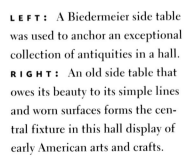

The kitchen table is more than a work surface. It is a latter-day harvest table, too, here groaning under the bounty of fresh produce. For kitchens that do not already boast a work island, an old table like this one can improve both the looks and the efficiency of the most popular room in the house. A shelf can be added below, between legs and stretchers, to provide more storage space.

An eat-in kitchen is the ideal for many families, and when it is as pretty as this one, a dining room is almost unnecessary. A wrought-iron trestle base on the table, folding French café-style chairs, and exposed below-counter shelves give the room an open, airy look.

For a classic country look, a wooden trestle table works well in an informal dining room. If you choose a trestle table for this purpose, though, make sure that the top extends far enough at each end to seat all of the diners comfortably.

ABOVE: When taken home from the office and painted, a desk serves as an effective display table for a dramatic floral centerpiece. **BELOW:** A pedestal desk with bombé lines and original floral designs becomes an elegant little writing table.

ABOVE: A black lacquer desk is a statement of drama and elegance in this artfully displayed tableau. **BELOW:** Of the many uses for old farm tables, one of the most popular is as the desk of a home office.

ABOVE: To add storage space and show off two country antiques, one bench has been set atop another. The bottom one serves as a bookcase, while the top one makes a convenient table. **BELOW:** A porch swing of painted wooden slats started out as a rustic bench.

ABOVE: Without hiding the ornamentation of the iron settee, pillows and a cushion have been added to create a comfortable spot in a porch alcove. **BELOW:** A cast-iron park bench, freshly painted, makes an imposing presence on the front porch.

ABOVE: A high-backed bench is an entry table and showcase for a quilt and a collection of jugs.
BELOW: Retrieved from the barn, a small bench once modified for holding tools now makes a handy vegetable bin.

ABOVE: A painted bench that never received an early decorator's finishing touches has been preserved on a country porch. **BELOW:** This painted bench, the width of the bed it serves, holds reading materials and sunflowers—and organizes shoes.

walls & wall displays

The quickest and easiest way to change a room is to paint or paper its walls, creating a uniform background for furnishings. Since many home interiors need repainting every few years, I feel I can afford to experiment freely. For most of my walls I choose white, just to keep things simple, but I love the effects that my friends have achieved with a little bit of paint and a lot of ingenuity. A wall doesn't have to recede into the back-ground. A bare wall makes a blank canvas for art, architecture, and col-lections. Trompe l'oeil renderings of classical motifs might be appropriate  in a stately sitting room; a collection of whimsical folk art would suit a country cottage interior. Any arrangement of plates, dolls, animal forms, or other objects can turn a wall into a three-dimensional art experience. Decorating a wall is not just a question of choosing paint and paper: when a wall is singled out for special treatment, the decor of the rest of the room should be taken into account.

PRECEDING PAGES: The decorative value of walls derives from their surface treatments, as simple as a custom paint finish, and from their function as a background for art, furnishings, and collections. **LEFT:** The classical motifs of a beautifully realized wall mural find their complement in an array of ornate candlesticks. **ABOVE:** An antique brocade remnant and a wrought-iron rod combine to create a dramatic wall hanging. **BELOW:** In an artist's nook, the wall is treated as a three-dimensional canvas, with abstract and figurative forms.

Decorative screens can be used as movable walls within a room. Here the photomural of a doge's palace in Venice helps to sustain the architectural theme present in this room. A screen of this dramatic intensity deserves to be seen on its own, rather than obscured behind any oversize furnishings.

A slab of ancient stone has been installed as a background for other fragments of the past and a chaste bowl of lilies and chrysanthemums. Walls with tactile values add their own decorative character to the room and can replace the more usual framed pictures and photographs.

The wall treatment in this room, conceived to exhibit a major collection, depends on a vivid yellow background color to help the blue-and-white ware stand out with unmistakable effect. When planning a room lined with shelves, remember that the floor area will be substantially reduced if the shelves are on all four sides.

A kitchen wall gains interest when treated differently above and below its chair rail. Wainscoting, or half-paneling, is often darker in a dining area, to obscure the scuff marks that occur when a chair backs up against the wall. A prized domestic vessel is given a prominent place at eye level in the room.

A serrated edge in the tilework gives pizzazz where an all-white tile backsplash and counter would have been bland. The echoing dark edges around the sink and on the counter help to make an artistic composition out of a plain kitchen wall.

To keep a clean, modern kitchen from becoming anti-septic, a playful checkerboard design was introduced in the tile wall, the same color as the ceiling fan and other decorative items. With its infinite potential for color and pattern, not to mention its washability, tile is an excellent covering for kitchen, bath, and courtyard.

A wall arrangement of folk art allows the viewer to appreciate the vivid portrayals of animal life against a neutral background.

An oversized roll of drawing paper mounted on the wall ensures an ever-changing panorama of art in this creative children's playroom.

Profiles of classical urns made from an inexpensive raw material provide a wall with a remarkably elegant collage.

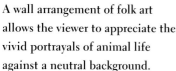

LEFT: In rooms lacking architectural interest, the use of a collection of bold patterns and colors, like this quartet of decorated ceramic plates, acts as a focal point. **RIGHT:** With the addition of picture rails at several different heights, a wall can serve as a changing gallery for personal collections.

A mural depicting a classical land-scape of rolling hills and columns with pediments makes a striking backdrop in this elegant entry hall.

To complete the effect after a stately old fireplace mantel was introduced into an interior wall, a trompe l'oeil painting was applied to create the illusion of a hearth.

The graphic Art Nouveau mosaic of a swan floating on sparkling water needs no help filling a wall with style.

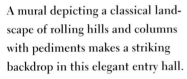

LEFT: The set of wall sconces, with their many reflecting panels for radiating candlelight, are the dominant element in an effective pyramidal decorating scheme for a wood cabinet. **RIGHT:** Architectural fragments have been arranged like a frieze above a wall niche where a carved angel perches dramatically.

ABOVE: Often the best treatment for a wall is to do nothing. The walls of this game room accentuate the rugged beauty of an old post-and-beam barn.
BELOW: The hand of a trompe l'oeil artist transforms a plain painted wood wall into a wildlife portrait.

ABOVE: For a formal, elegant room, nothing is quite as successful as a beautiful wallpaper. **BELOW:** A festive, break-the-rules wall treatment helps a small galley kitchen feel more spacious than it really is.

ABOVE: A mirror, given its own border on the wall, becomes as emphatic a work of art as the framed drawing of an urn. **BELOW:** A sampler of dried herbs and flowers brings the garden into the house.

ABOVE: Used as wall covering, this venerable tapestry helps to transform the corner of a room into an unofficial shrine. **BELOW:** Nineteenth-century children's dresses and accessories unexpectedly decorate a bathroom wall.

Displaying collections in their entirety can give endless interest to a room, especially in a country-style decor. Here an arrangement of framed and unframed collectibles achieves a unified visual impact on one wall, while on the other a peg rack shows off a group of antique baskets.

A Lutyens-design garden bench looks to be in its own element inside the house, thanks to the inspired renderings of scenes familiar in the growing season. In very small enclosed spaces, a mural of an outdoor scene can relieve the feeling of claustrophobia.

The vivid textural surfaces of Native American weavings, hung on a wall, are used to display a collection of kachina dolls. Fabrics are not only an attractive alternative to wallpaper, they are also practical. They muffle sound, can be taken down and cleaned, and can be used for changing displays without patching nail holes in the wall.

ABOVE: The subtle stripe pattern of the wall covering makes the arrangement of four botanical prints stand out more prominently. **BELOW:** In this room the wall itself is the art, in the form of a faux marble surface and shells set in concrete.

ABOVE: A wall decoration resembling priestly vestments is an unusual backdrop for a group of small collectibles. **BELOW:** A collection of identically framed industrial prints was hung on painted wood walls from floor to ceiling.

windows

Window treatments can be plain, pretty, strictly functional, or elaborate, depending on many factors, including the view through the window, the architectural style, if any, of the window, and the role of the window in the interior design of the room. Where natural light exists, windows should always be used to enjoy it. Adding a skylight window can transform a small, dark bathroom into a pleasurable spa. Old leaded or stained-glass windows can be installed in any room to add character where none exists. A Palladian or Gothic window may be so beautiful on its own that little if any window dressing is called for. But most windows benefit from some form of decorative treatment—a finishing touch as simple

as a panel of lace, providing privacy but letting in light, or a recycled printed tablecloth from a vintage 1940s kitchen. One of my favorite treatments uses a branch as a curtain rod; in another, rubber bands gather fabric into rosettes at the curtain corners.

PRECEDING PAGES: With or without embellishment, windows are an important architectural element in the rooms of a house, a source of natural light and an inherent focal point. **LEFT:** The leaded and beveled glass in the doors, transom, and landing windows is so distinctive it has been left uncovered. **ABOVE:** A lace swag treatment gives a Victorian flourish to an ordinary six-over-six window. **BELOW:** Colorful kitchen linens from the 1940s have been recycled as kitschy unmatched curtains complete with novelty tiebacks.

Floor-length curtains of voluminous gathered fabric and a valance cut on an angle produce a soft, romantic look on a window.

An asymmetrical swag and jabot curtain treatment, tied in a casual fashion, dresses up a bedroom window while permitting the maximum amount of light.

The horizontal pattern of louvered shutters gives a plain geometric look. Popular in the South, louvers can be manipulated to shut out light and heat but let in air.

LEFT: The use of cording, tassels, and tiebacks gives a decorative flourish, in this case one with a seashell theme, to a window treatment. **RIGHT:** Modern window design brings light into a house in many shapes and forms. When thinking of light, remember the dramatic effects of shadows.

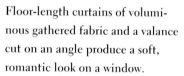

A simple tab curtain befits a country interior, but it is the choice of paint color that gives the window its style.

Sheer fabric lends its grace and verve to a window without darkening the room.

When lace is hung at a window, it projects intriguing shadows into the room and lends a romantic air to the exterior view.

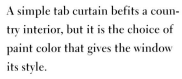

LEFT: Windows with extraordinary views are best left uncovered when privacy is not a concern. **RIGHT:** A wall of Palladian-style French doors, free of adornment, is the principal focal point in a country sunroom.

ABOVE: A formal interior includes a lavish silk taffeta valance and curtain over sheer fabric and window shade. **BELOW:** Standard sash windows were transformed into a room's center of interest with the addition of a half-round with a sunburst motif.

ABOVE: The sheer fabric used to cover the French doors has been hung to create an elegant treatment at the top. **BELOW:** Six-over-six paned windows, crowned by a half-round, give an old-fashioned farmhouse look to a new kitchen.

ABOVE: The skylight in a passageway becomes a point of interest with the addition of brightly painted struts. **BELOW:** Along with admitting light into closed quarters, this skylight window permits ventilation and offers a celestial view.

ABOVE: A bay window with ivy trained to define its shape has been decorated with soft cushions and pillows in lively complementary fabrics. **BELOW:** Shutters with movable louvers allow privacy when needed or as much softly filtered light as desired.

ABOVE: A shutter with a built-in silhouette adds its exotic note to a room with foreign intrigue. **BELOW:** Lace veils a bay window with romance and pattern, offering privacy but admitting sunshine.

ABOVE: A valance of canvas tacked to the window framework with brass studs provides a tailored top treatment for this window. **BELOW:** The window seat is furnished to coordinate with the main room, with paisley curtains that echo the peeled bark motif.

ABOVE: Café curtains evoke the traditional, and the leopard-skin valance the innovative. **BELOW:** This lonely attic window gets some attention when timeworn family possessions are deliberately arranged around it.

ABOVE: In a treatment as simple as a handkerchief in a breast pocket, a small amount of fabric gives a window a large amount of style. **BELOW:** An arched Gothic window is flanked by plain shutters.

A deep-silled window in a traditional dining room is dressed with sheer curtains that do not interfere with the light or the view.

A curtain rod found in the woods can be harnessed for window decoration in a room like this with primitive qualities.

Furnished with a comfortable seat and pillow, an alcove graced by a beautiful Gothic window becomes a tiny room for contemplation.

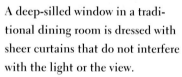

LEFT: The window set in the thick wall of an adobe house is the centerpiece in an arrangement of precious possessions. **RIGHT:** The hard surface of the horizontal blind window treatment is softened by a natural curtain of ivy and a spherical objet d'art.

The bold floral pattern of vintage fabric has been adapted as a swag and jabot treatment, making it the dominant accent in the room.

The antique leaded glass window was salvaged and reinstalled over a kitchen sink where it could be fully appreciated.

Dressing a narrow window with a single curtain tied to one side creates the illusion of greater width.

LEFT: A recessed window, given definition by its painted trim, provides contrast to the unusual polka dot wall treatment. **RIGHT:** Beveled and leaded glass lifts window fashions to an art form that defies further embellishment.

directory

This buying guide features stores, suppliers, and manufacturers that will help you find the perfect decorating details for your home. Ask your interior designer or contractor to contact the wholesale-only listings.

bowls & baskets

Williams-Sonoma
100 Northpoint Street
San Francisco, CA 94133
800-541-1262
Kitchen bowls and accessories. Catalog.

Pottery Barn
P.O. Box 7044
San Francisco, CA
94120-7044
800-922-5507
Bowls, baskets, home furnishings. Catalog.

Pier 1 Imports
P.O. Box 962030
Fort Worth, TX 76161-0020
800-447-4371
Bowls, baskets, home furnishings and accessories. Catalog.

Palacek
P.O. Box 225
Richmond, CA 94808-0225
800-274-7730
Baskets, furnishings, accessories. Wholesale.

Thru the Grapevine
3149 State Route 133
P.O. Box 250
Bethel, OH 45106
513-734-2710
Baskets, grapevine wreaths. Wholesale/retail.

Lady Slipper Designs
Route 3, Box 556
Bemidji, MN 56601
218-751-0763
Birch-bark baskets made by northern Minnesota Ojibwe Indians. Wholesale.

Cabin Creek Farm
Hannah and Art Stearns
P.O. Box 22
Mount Sherman, KY 42764
502-932-6227
Large selection of baskets, mostly antiques.

Hearth and Home Designs
7541 Woodman Place
Van Nuys, CA 91405
818-780-9242
Large serving bowls and kitchen accessories. Wholesale.

Los Angeles Pottery
1936 Pontius Avenue
Los Angeles, CA 90025
310-575-1418
Hand-painted, oven-proof, lead-free bowls and dinnerware. Wholesale.

Monroe Salt Works
Stovepipe Alley
Monroe, ME 04951
207-525-4471
Salt-glazed stoneware.
Wholesale/retail.

Dean & Deluca
560 Broadway
New York, NY 10012
212-431-1691
Home accessories and
gourmet foods.
Wholesale/retail.

Basketry and Crafts by Karen
405 Laurel Lane
Madison, IN 47250
812-265-6164
Handmade Appalachian-style
baskets and wreaths made
from all-natural elements.
Wholesale.

Rowe Pottery Works
404 England Street
Cambridge, WI 53523
800-356-5003
Salt-glazed pottery.
Wholesale/retail.

Fishs Eddy
889 Broadway
New York, NY 10003
212-420-9020

Industrial china for the
home.

Jefferson General Store
113 E. Austin
Jefferson, TX 75657
903-665-8481
Pottery, antiques, gifts, country store and nostalgia items.
Wholesale/retail.

Gordon Foster
1322 Third Avenue
New York, NY 10021
212-744-4922
Home accessories.

beds

Baker Furniture Company
1660 Monroe Avenue NW
Grand Rapids, MI 49505
616-361-7321
Large selection of styles and
collections. Wholesale.

Lexington Furniture
Company
P.O. Box 1008
Lexington, NC 27293
704-249-5300
Carries Mary Emmerling's
"American Country West"
furniture line. Wholesale.

Simply Southern Furniture
P.O. Box 370
Industrial Blvd.
Toccoa, GA 30577
706-886-7454
Country-designed beds.
Wholesale.

Broyhill Furniture Industries
1 Broyhill Park
Lenoir, NC 28633
704-758-3111
Modern, contemporary,
country, southwestern design.
Wholesale.

The Lane Company, Inc.
East Franklin Avenue
P.O. Box 151
Altavista, VA 24517
804-369-5641
Country collections, lacquer,
contemporary. Wholesale.

American Star Buck
P.O. Box 15376
Lenexa, KS 66215
913-894-1567
Pencil-post reproductions in
pine, oak, maple, cherry,
mahogany, ash, and walnut.

Country Affaire/Elden
Collection
1170 North Main
Orange, CA 92667
714-771-5999
Wood/iron combination
with coordinating colors.
Wholesale.

Vermont Tubbs
P.O. Box 148
Forestdale, VT 05745
800-327-7026
Beds hand-crafted out of
hardwood ash. Wholesale.

Yesteryear Wicker
P.O. Box 384
Clinton, MD 20735
301-868-7781
Rattan and wicker beds.
Wholesale.

Portico Bed & Bath
139 Spring Street
New York, NY 10012
212-343-2230
Wrought-iron, cast-iron beds,
plus linens.

dressers, dressing tables & mirrors

Union City Mirror &
  Table Co.
129 34th Street
Box 825
Union City, NJ 07087
Dressing tables, mirrors,
French provincial design.
Wholesale.

Crate in Motion Furniture
3605 Virginia Beach Blvd.
Virginia Beach, VA 23452
804-431-1333
Solid-wood dressers and
chests of drawers.

American Mirror Company
Galax, VA 24333
703-236-5111
Contemporary and tradi-
tional styles. Wholesale.

Amish Country Collection
RD 5, Sunset Valley Road
New Castle, PA 16105
412-458-4811
Hand-painted, custom-
designed, hickory-branch
mirrors. Wholesale/retail.

Carver's Guild
Cannery Row
P.O. Box 198
West Groton, MA 01472
800-445-3464
Decorative mirrors.
Wholesale.

Carolina Mirror Co.
P.O. Box 548
North Wilkesboro, NC 28659
919-838-2151
Unframed and decorative
mirrors. Wholesale.

Friedman Bros. Decorative
  Arts, Inc.
9015 NW 105 Way
Medley, FL 33178
305-887-3170
Manufactured framed mir-
rors. Wholesale.

Brentwood Manor
Furnishings
316 Virginia Avenue
Clarksville, VA 23927
804-374-4297
Variety of dressers, dressing
tables, mirrors.

Thomasville Furniture
  Industries
P.O. Box 339
Thomasville, NC 27361-0339
919-472-4000
Large collections of dressers,
dressing tables. Wholesale.

Boyd Furniture Company
6355 Washington Blvd.
Los Angeles, CA 90040
213-726-6767
Contemporary dressers.
Wholesale.

British Khaki Home
  Furnishings
214 W. 39th Street
New York, NY 10018
212-221-1199
Variety of dressers, dressing
tables. By appointment only.

tables, benches &
desks

Yield House
P.O. Box 5000
North Conway, NH
03860-5000
800-258-4720
Shaker design, benches,
tables. Catalog.

The Roudebush Co.
Main Street
P.O. Box 348
Star City, IN 46985
800-847-4947
Buckboard benches.
Wholesale/retail.

Ron Fisher's Furniture
1001 South 18th Avenue
Marshalltown, IA 50158
800-231-7370
Painted pine furniture.
Wholesale.

General Store
7920 NW 76th Avenue
Medley, FL 33166
404-577-8270
Country design furnishings.
Wholesale.

Martinek Designs
4535 Travis at Knox
Dallas, TX 75205
800-852-9712
Hand-carved, hand-crafted,
country French designs.
Wholesale.

Maine Cottage Furniture
P.O. Box 935
Lower Falls Landing
Yarmouth, ME 04096
207-846-3699
Colorful and fun furniture.

Winsome Trading, Inc.
7023 NE 175th Street
Bothell, WA 98011
206-483-8888
Beech tables and benches
imported from Thailand.
Wholesale.

chairs & sofas

Union City Chair Company
18 Market Street
Union City, PA 16438
814-438-3878
Wood chairs in various styles
and sizes. Wholesale.

Tell City Chair Company
P.O. Box 369
Tell City, IN 47586
812-547-3491
Solid wood chairs in various
styles and sizes. Wholesale.

La-Z-Boy Chair Co.
1284 N. Telegraph Road
Monroe, MI 48161
800-THEN-RELAX
Largest U.S. manufacturer
of upholstered furniture.
Wholesale.

Pier 1 Imports
P.O. Box 962030
Fort Worth, TX 76161-0020
800-447-4371
Upholstered and wicker
chairs and sofas. Catalog.

Lee Industries Inc.
P.O. Box 26
Newton, NC 28658
704-464-8318
Upholstered sofas and chairs.
Wholesale.

Hickory Chair Company
37 9th Street Pl. SE
Hickory, NC 28603
704-328-1801
Upholstered sofas and chairs.
Wholesale.

Edgar B.
P.O. Box 849
3550 Highway 158
Clemmons, NC 27012
800-628-3808

Represents over 200 furniture
manufacturers. Catalog.

Ethan Allen, Inc.
Ethan Allen Drive
P.O. Box 1966
Danbury, CT 06813-1966
203-743-8000
Upholstered chairs, sofas and
other fine home furnishings.
Wholesale.

Pearson Company
1420 Progress Street
P.O. Box 2838
Highpoint, NC 27261
919-882-8135
Upholstered chairs, sofas.
Wholesale.

Palecek
P.O. Box 225
Richmond, CA 94808-0225
800-274-7730
Wicker chairs, love seats and
accessories. Wholesale.

Shabby Chic Furniture
1013 Montana Avenue
Santa Monica, CA 90404
310-394-1975
Oversized furniture with
machine-washable slipcovers.

Marion Travis
P.O. Box 1041
Statesville, NC 28687
704-528-4424
Ladder-back chairs in a variety of sizes.

Coming to America
276 Lafayette Street
New York, NY 10012
212-343-2968
Sofa and chairs designed by
David Drummond.

Home James . . . Now!
55 Main Street
Easthampton, NY 11937
516-324-2307
Traditional, classic styles.
Open spring and summer
only.

George Smith Sofas and
  Chairs
73 Spring Street
New York, NY 10012
212-226-4747
Handmade English furniture.
Wholesale/retail.

ABC Carpet & Home
888 Broadway
New York, NY 10003
212-473-3000
Huge selection of old and
new items, including accessories.

Zona
97 Greene Street
New York, NY 10012
212-925-6750
Southwest and Italian
designs.

Wolfman Gold & Good
  Company
116 Greene Street
New York, NY 10012
212-431-1888
Home furnishings, acces-
sories.

Barton Sharpe, Ltd.
119 Spring Street
New York, NY 10012
212-925-9562
        or
71 Buckram Road
Locust Valley, NY 11560
516-674-8605
Windsor, Chippendale, and
Queen Anne chairs.

Distant Origin
153 Mercer Street
New York, NY 10012
212-941-0024
Mexican Mennonite coaches,
sofas, antique contemporary
chairs.

c.i.t.e.
100 Wooster Street
New York, NY 10012
212-431-7272
Antique chairs as well as
other antique pieces.

flowers & garden elements

Wolfman Gold & Good
  Company
116 Greene Street
New York, NY 10012
212-431-1888
Birdhouses, antique flower
buckets, gardening tools.

Two Rivers Garden, Inc.
1833 St. Mary's Road
Villa Ridge, MO 63089
800-648-0461
Birdhouses, floral accessories
with bird themes. Wholesale.

Opus Incorporated
P.O. Box 525
Bellingham, MA 02019-0525
Bird feeders, ceramic acces-
sories. Wholesale. Catalog.

W. Atlee Burpee & Co.
300 Park Avenue
Warminster, PA 18974
215-674-4900
Seeds, bulbs, garden supplies.
Catalog.

Flowers Forever
311 East 61st Street
New York, NY 10021
212-308-0088
Dried flower arrangements,
supplies for the do-it-your-
selfer. Wholesale/retail.

Wells Lamont
6640 West Touhy Avenue
Niles, IL 60714-4587
800-323-2830
Yard and gardening gloves.
Catalog.

Elizabeth Street Garden &
  Gallery
210 Elizabeth Street
New York, NY 10012
212-941-4800

Garden statues, gazebos, furniture, fountains. Wholesale/retail.

John Scheepers, Inc.
P.O. Box 700
Bantam, CT 06750
203-567-0838
Flower bulbs.

Melnor, Inc.
One Carol Place
Moonachie, NJ 07074-1386
201-641-5000
Hoses, sprinklers, humidifiers. Catalog.

Calyx & Corolla
1550 Bryant Street #900
San Francisco, CA 94103
800-800-7788
Large selection of flowers and arrangements.

Alsto's Handy Helpers
P.O. Box 1267
Galesburg, IL 61401
800-447-0048
Home, yard, and garden tools. Catalog.

Breck's
US Reservation Center
6523 North Galena Road
Peoria, IL 61632
Flower bulbs. Catalog.

Country Gardener
491 West State Road 114
North Manchester, IN 46962
219-982-4707
Unique birdhouses, garden ornaments, herbs, everlastings. Wholesale/retail.

Lexington Gardens
1011 Lexington Avenue
New York, NY 10021
212-861-4390
Decorative gardening elements, furnishings, dried flower arrangements.

Devonshire
Main Street
Bridgehampton, NY 11932
516-537-2661
Period and decorative garden accessories. Open April to November.

Devonshire
340 Worth Avenue
Palm Beach, FL 33480
407-833-0796

Period and decorative garden accessories.

David Kay
One Jenni Lane
Peoria, IL 61614-3198
800-535-9917
Garden accessories, furniture, wall decorations. Catalog.

Gardener's Eden
P.O. Box 7307
San Francisco, CA
94120-7307
800-822-9600
Garden accessories. Catalog.

Jackson & Perkins
85 Rose Lane
Medford, OR 97501
800-292-4769
Bulbs, roses, perennials, gift items, accessories. Catalog.

Two's Company
33 Bertel Avenue
Mount Vernon, NY 10550
914-664-2277
Flower containers. Wholesale. Catalog.

Lloyd/Flanders Industries
3010 Tenth Street
P.O. Box 500
Menominee, MI 49858
800-526-9894
Indoor/outdoor wicker
furniture.

New Budoff Corporation
East Broadway
P.O. Box 530
Monticello, NY 12701
800-548-0204
Solid-oak Adirondack furni-
ture. Wholesale.

Rooms & Gardens
290 Lafayette Street
New York, NY 10012
212-431-1297
Garden antiques, furniture,
accessories.

Marston-Luce
1314 21st Street NW
Washington, DC 20036
202-775-9460
Antiques, birdbaths, urns,
statues, tools.

Adirondack Designs
350 Cypress Street
Fort Bragg, CA 95437
800-222-0343
Adirondack furniture, arbors,
redwood benches.

Willsboro Wood Products
P.O. Box 509
South Au Sable Street
Keeseville, NY 12944
518-834-5200 (NY state)
800-342-3373 (outside NY)
Planters, benches,
Adirondack furniture.
Wholesale/retail.

Moultrie Manufacturing
 Company
P.O. Box 1179
Moultrie, GA 31776
800-841-8674
Cast-aluminum indoor/out-
door furniture.
Wholesale/retail.

Wood Classics Inc.
Osprey Lane
Gardiner, NY 12525
914-255-5599
Teak and mahogany tables
and chairs, planters, mission
furniture, and British,
Chippendale, and Georgian
benches.

candles & candle holders

Design Ideas
Box 2967
Springfield, IL 62708
217-753-3081
Candleholders. Wholesale.

Firelight Glass
1000 42nd Street
Emeryville, CA 94608-3621
510-428-0607
Hand-blown glass oil candles.
Wholesale/retail.

Yankee Candle Co.
Route 5
South Deerfield, MA 01373
413-665-8306
Tapers, tumblers, pillars,
tealights in a variety of scents
and sizes. Wholesale/retail.

Wolfman Gold & Good
 Company
116 Greene Street
New York, NY 10012
212-431-1888
Candles, candelabra.

E. Harcourt's
68 Palmer Avenue
Bronxville, NY 10708
914-779-2819
Aroma-therapy candles.
Wholesale/retail.

lamps & lighting

George Kovacs Lighting, Inc.
67-25 Otto Road
Glendale, NY 11385
718-628-5201
Halogen, swing arm, primitive designs, table lamps.
Wholesale/retail.

Renovator's Supply Co.
Renovator's Old Mill
Millers Falls, MA 01349
413-659-2241
Period lighting in brass.
Catalog.

Alsy Lighting
One Early Street
Ellwood City, PA 16117
412-758-0707
Portable, table and floor
lamps. Wholesale/retail.

Nora Fenton, Inc.
107 Trumbull Street
Elizabeth, NJ 07206
908-351-5460

Coordinated lamps and
accessories. Wholesale.

Wildwood Lamps & Accents
P.O. Box 672
Rocky Mount, NC 27802
919-446-3266
Table and floor lamps, chandeliers in porcelain, brass,
pewter. Wholesale.

Currey & Company
200 Ottley Drive
Atlanta, GA 30327
404-885-1444
Wrought-iron, wood-base,
stone-base lamps, chandeliers. Wholesale.

Meyda Tiffany
1123 Stark Street
Utica, NY 13502
315-797-8775
Tiffany-designed lamps.
Wholesale/retail.

Shady Lady's, Inc.
P.O. Box 1
Cedarburg, WI 53012
414-377-6848
Iron and ceramic bases with
decorative paper shades.
Wholesale.

antiques, collections, wall displays, racks, shelves & cupboards

Rancho
322 McKenzie Street
Santa Fe, NM 87501
505-986-1688
Vintage cowboy and Western
memorabilia.

Wild Goose Chase
1936 South Coast Highway
Laguna Beach, CA 92651
714-376-9388
Antique Americana including
quilts, beacon blankets, pre-1900 antiques, and painted
furniture.

America Hurrah
766 Madison Avenue
New York, NY 10021
212-535-1930
Antiques, including quilts,
American folk art, and Native
American art.

Casa El Patio
38 Newtown Lane
Easthampton, NY 11937
516-329-0300
McCoy pottery, candles,
antique painted furniture
and accessories.

Charlotte Moss & Co.
1027 Lexington Avenue
New York, NY 10021
212-772-3320
Home furnishings, decorative
accessories, pillows, porcelain, china, old books, lamps.

Cherishables
1608 20th Street NW
Washington, DC 20009
202-785-4087
Antique accessories, plus new
items for entertaining and
tabletop.

Claiborne Gallery
452 West Broadway
New York, NY 10012
212-475-3072
Antique accessories, country
furniture, iron furniture.

Distant Origin
153 Mercer Street
New York, NY 10012
212-941-0024
China, antique benches,
tables, accessories, and gifts.

Nancy Thomas Gallery
P.O. Box 274
Yorktown, VA 23690
804-898-3665
American-made 18th-
century/early-19th-century
antiques. Wholesale/retail.

EGH Peter, Inc.
Box 52
Norfolk, CT 06058
203-542-5221
American 18th- and 19th-
century painted furniture,
with an emphasis on original
finishes. By appointment
only.

East Meets West Antiques
658 North Larchmont Blvd.
Hollywood, CA 90004
213-461-1389
Antiques, accessories, quilts,
textiles, country furnishings.
Wholesale/retail.

Laura Fisher/Antique Quilts
 and Americana
1050 Second Avenue
Gallery 84
New York, NY 10022
212-838-2596
Antique quilts, hooked rugs,
beacon blankets, textiles,
accessories. Wholesale/retail.

Lewis Keister Antiques
209 Market Street
Lewisburg, PA 17837
717-523-3945
Textiles, quilts, accessories.
Wholesale/retail.

Room Service by Ann Fox
4354 Lover's Lane
Dallas, TX 75225
214-369-7666
Antique beds, great new
fabrics, paintings, vintage
memorabilia.

Stars Antique Mall
7027 SE Milwaukee Avenue
Portland, OR 97202
503-239-0346
Antiques, collectibles, and
extraordinary junk.

Gaglio & Molnar, Inc.
Box 375
Wurtsboro, NY 12790
914-888-5077
Antiques, furniture, accessories, American folk art. By appointment only.

Home Town
131 Wooster Street
New York, NY 10012
212-674-5770
American antiques.

Hope and Wilder Home
454 Broome Street
New York, NY 10013
212-966-9010
Antique cupboards, accessories, new sofas, chairs, and ottomans, vintage and new fabrics.

Kelter-Malce Antiques
74 Jane Street
New York, NY 10014
212-675-7380
American Indian art, textiles, quilts, hooked rugs, folk art.

Susan Parrett/Rod Lich
2164 Canal Lane
Georgetown, IN 47122
812-951-3454

Antiques. By appointment only.

Bert Savage Larch Lodge
Route126
Center Strafford, NH 03815
603-269-7411
Antique rustic furniture and accessories, antique canoes. By appointment only.

Linda and Howard Stein
Route 202, P.O. Box 11
Lahaska, PA 18931
215-297-0606
Antiques, decorative accessories, folk art. Wholesale/retail.

Sammy's
484 Broome Street
New York, NY 10013
212-343-2357
Antiques, Americana,19th-century tools, good junk.

Lost City Arts
275 Lafayette Street
New York, NY 10012
212-941-8025
Antiques and 20th-century decorative and architectural artifacts.

Bertha Black
80 Thompson Street
New York, NY 10012
212-966-7116
Antique accessories, specializing in folk art, painted furniture, religious art, American glass, English ceramics, textiles.

LS
469 West Broadway
New York, NY 10012
212-673-4575
Home, personal, and executive accessories, tabletop, giftware.

Henro
525 Broome Street
New York, NY 10013
212-343-0221
Primitive antique furniture, old toys, McCoy pottery, Bauer pottery, silver hotel plates.

Joel Mathieson
190 Sixth Avenue
New York, NY 10013
212-941-1491
Victorian, medieval, pre-Columbian, eclectic collections. Wholesale/retail.

David & Co.
192 Sixth Avenue
New York, NY 10013
Decorative antiques, mirrors, lamps, small tables, 30's and 40's pottery. Wholesale/retail.

Hinton & Company
108 Wooster Street
New York, NY 10012
212-343-2430
Contemporary collectibles, gift items, antiques.

Susan P. Meisel Decorative Arts
133 Prince Street
New York, NY 10012
212-254-0137
Collections, sailboats, jewelry, Clarice Cliff pottery.

Cynthia Beneduce Art & Antiques
99 East 4th Street
New York, NY 10003
212-982-3185
Primitive garden furniture and architectural pieces. By appointment only.

Brian Windsor Art & Antiques
281 Lafayette Street
New York, NY 10012
212-274-0411
Primitive garden furniture, architectural pieces.

architectural elements, floors, stairs, doors, windows & mantels

Urban Archeology
Route 27
Bridgehampton, NY 11932
516-537-0124
          or
285 Lafayette Street
New York, NY 10012
212-431-6969
Stairs, windows, lighting, sinks, tubs, garden furniture.

Armstrong World Industries
P.O. Box 3001
Lancaster, PA 17604
800-233-3823
Floor and ceiling products. Manufacturer.

American Olean Tile Co.
1000 Cannon Avenue
Lansdale, PA 19446
215-855-1111

Ceramic tile for floors and walls. Manufacturer.

Chadsworth Columns
P.O. Box 53268
Atlanta, GA 30355
404-876-5410
Architectural columns, mantels, pedestals, table bases. Manufacturer.

World of Moulding
3103 South Main Street
Santa Ana, CA 92707
714-556-7772
Moldings, mantels, staircases, fretwork. Wholesale/retail.

NMC/Focal Point
P.O. Box 93327
Atlanta, GA 30377
404-351-0820
Moldings, chair rails, columns, doorways, window/wall treatments, ceiling rosettes, recessed domes. Manufacturer.

Classic Architectural
  Specialties
3223 Canton Street
Dallas, TX 75226
214-748-1668
Columns, corbels, brackets,
moldings, tin ceilings,
appliqués.

The Old Wagon Factory
103 Russell Street
P.O. Box 1247
Clarksville, VA 23927
804-374-5787
Doors, friezes, medallions,
Victorian porch furniture.
Catalog.

Georgia-Pacific
133 Peachtree St. NE
Atlanta, GA 30303
404-652-6227
All kinds of home building
products. Manufacturer.

AJ Stairs, Inc.
195 Drum Point Road
Brick, NJ 08723
908-477-8080
Stairs. Manufacturer.

Goddard Stairs
P.O. Box 502
Logan, KS 67646
913-689-4341
Stairs. Manufacturer.

Vintage Woodworks
Highway 34 South
P.O. Box R
Quinlan, TX 75474
903-356-2158
Architectural details, brack-
ets, corbels, cornices, mold-
ings, gables.
Wholesale/retail.

Fypon Molded Millwork
22 West Pennsylvania
  Avenue
Stewartstown, PA 17363
717-993-2593
Columns, brackets, moldings,
door entries, shutters.
Manufacturer.

Peachtree Doors and
  Windows
P.O. Box 5700
Norcross, GA 30091
404-497-2000
Interior and exterior doors;
wood and aluminum win-
dows. Manufacturer.

Elegant Entries
240 Washington Street
Auburn, MA 01501
508-832-9898
Mahogany, rosewood, teak
and oak doors.
Wholesale/retail.

Bend Door Co.
62845 Boyd Acres Road
Bend, OR 97701
503-385-1422
Fir doors. Manufacturer.

Morgan Manufacturing
601 Oregon Street
P.O. Box 2446
Oshkosh, WI 54903
414-235-7170
Oak, fir, pine doors in all
styles. Manufacturer.

Hartco
Tibbols Flooring Company
P.O. Box 4009
Oneida, TN 37841
615-569-8526
Oak wood flooring.
Manufacturer.

Bruce Hardwood Floors
4255 LBJ Freeway
Dallas, TX 75234
214-931-3100
Oak, maple wood flooring.
Manufacturer.

Caradco
P.O. Box 920
Rantoul, IL 61866
217-893-4444
Pine wood windows and
doors. Manufacturer.

Marvin Windows & Doors
2020 Silver Bell Road
Suite 15
Eagan, MN 55122
612-452-3039
Wood windows and doors.
Manufacturer.

Country Floors
15 East 16th Street
New York, NY 10003
212-627-8300
Ceramic tiles for floors
and walls.

Harris-Tarkett, Inc.
P.O. Box 300
Johnson City, TN 37605
615-928-3122
Red oak, ash, white oak,
walnut wood flooring.
Manufacturer.

English Country Antiques
Snake Hollow Road
Bridgehamtpon, NY 11932
516-537-0606
Antique doors and home
furnishings.

Seret & Sons
149 East Alameda
Santa Fe, NM 87501
505-988-9151
Doors, architectural details,
rugs, custom furniture.
Wholesale/retail.

Cherishables
1608 20th Street NW
Washington, DC 20009
202-785-4087
Mantels, windows.

Marston-Luce
1314 21st Street NW
Washington, DC 20036
202-775-9460
Architectural details,
columns, windows.

Heritage Mantels, Inc.
P.O. Box 240
Southport, CT 06490
203-335-0552
Marble reproduction man-
tels. Manufacturer.

Readybuilt Products
 Company
P.O. Box 4425
Baltimore, MD 21223
410-233-5833
Mantels, electric logs,
andirons. Manufacturer.

index

photograph credits

Code: Numbers indicate pages. T—Top; TR—Top Right; TL—Top Left; TC—Top Center; C—Center; R—Right; L—Left; B—Bottom; BR—Bottom Right; BL—Bottom Left; BC—Bottom Center.

CLAY, LANGDON: 2BL, BR; 8BL, BR; 11; 12B; 13; 16; 20C; 23TL; 24TC; 30TL, BL; 31TL; 33BR; 34C, B; 35B; 38; 41C; 47T; 49; 57TL; 60; 63TL, TR; 64TL, TR; 65T; 67TL; 70-72; 73T; 74TC; 79BL, BR; 80TL, TR; 81TL; 85T; 87TL; 89C; 97TL; 98BR; 106TL; 130TR; 138BL, BR; 142T; 143BR; 150TC; 151TC; 155TL, TR; 163BL; 164B; 178T; 179BL; 192. **GREENE, JOSHUA:** 3; 14; 15; 17; 18TL, BL; 19TL, BL; 20T, B; 21; 22; 24TL, BR; 25TC, BL; 26; 28; 29; 31TR, BR; 32; 33TL, TR; 34T; 35T; 36; 37; 39; 40C, B; 41T, B; 42TR, TL, BL; 43TR, BL, BR; 44TL, TC, TR, BR; 45TL, TC, TR, BR; 46; 47C; 48; 50; 51; 52T, C; 53C, B; 54BL, BR; 55; 57TC, BL, BR; 59; 61; 62; 64 BL; 65C; 67BR; 68; 69C; 74BR; 75TR, BL, BR; 76TR, BR; 78BL, BR; 81TR, BL, BR; 82; 84; 85B; 86TL, TR, BL, BR; 87TC, BL, BR; 88; 89T; 90T; 91TC, BL; 93; 95T, B; 96TR; 98TL, TR, BL; 99; 100BL; 101BR; 102; 103; 105B; 106TC, TR, BL, BR; 107TL, TC; 108BL; 109BR; 110TL, TR, BL; 111TL; 114; 115B, 116TC, TR, BL; 117TC, BR; 118; 119TL, BR; 120BL, BR; 121TL, TC, TR; 122C, B; 123B; 127B; 128TL, TC; 130BL; 131B; 133TL, BL, BR; 139TR; 140T, C; 141; 142B; 143TR; 144; 146; 147; 148C; 149T, C; 150TR, BL, BR; 151BR; 152TL, TR, BL; 153TC, TR, BL, BR; 154TL, TR, BR; 155TC; 156; 159B; 160TL, BL, BR; 161TR, BL; 162TL, TR, BL; 163TR, BR; 164T, C; 165TL, BL; 166 BL, BR; 167TL, BL, BR; 168; 170; 173T, B; 174TL, TC, BR; 175TC; 176TL, BL; 177BL; 178B; 179TL, BR; 183B; 184; 185TL, TC, TR; 186BL, BR; 187BL; 188TR, BL; 189TL, TR, BR; 190TR, BR; 191TL, TC, TR, BR. **HALL, JOHN:** 25BR; 56B; 67BL; 74TL; 77B; 78TL; 80TC; 87TR; 97TR; 98TC; 100TR; 113; 115T; 116TL, BR; 117TL, TR, BL; 121BR; 122T; 128TR; 132TL; 133TR; 137B; 138TL; 139TL; 159T; 162TC; 165BR; 166TR; 167TR. **McNAMARA, JEFFREY:** 18BR; 25TR; 35C; 45BL; 111TR; 119BL; 132BR; 137T; 139BL; 182; 183T. **MEAD, CHRIS:** 2BC; 8TL, TR; 12T; 19TR; 24TR; 44BL; 52B; 57TR; 65B; 69T; 76TL; 80BL, BR; 81TC; 89B; 96TL; 96BL, BR; 107TR; 110BR; 111BL, BR; 128BL; 133TC; 174BL; 177BR; 178C; 189BL; 190TC. **SAMUELSON, JEREMY:** 23TC; 25TL; 83; 86TC; 91TL; 100BR; 127T; 129BL; 130BR; 132TC, TR, BL; 153TL; 171T; 175TR. **SKOTT, MICHAEL:** 19TC, BR; 24 BL; 27; 30TR, BR; 31BL; 33BL; 40T; 47B; 56C; 63 BR; 66BL; 73B; 74TR; 75TL, TC; 76 BL; 77T; 79TL; 90B; 91TR, BR; 108BR; 112; 136; 139BR; 140B; 148C; 149B; 155BR; 157; 158; 161BR; 163TC; 166TL; 172B; 173C; 176 TR; 180; 185BR; 187TR; 188BR; 190TL; 191BL. **STREET-PORTER, TIM:** 1; 5*; 8TC; 10; 18TR; 23TR; 53T; 54TL, TR; 58; 63TC, BL; 66TL, TR, BR; 74BL; 78TR; 79TR*; 92; 97BL; 100TL; 101TL*, TR; 104; 105T; 107BL, BR; 108TR, TL*; 109TL, TR*; 124; 125; 126; 128BR; 129TL, TR, BR; 130TL*; 131T; 134; 135; 138TR; 143TL*, BL; 145*; 148T; 150TL; 151TL, TR, BL; 152BR; 154BL; 155BL; 160TR; 161TL; 162BR*; 163TL; 165TR; 169; 171B; 172T*, C; 174TR; 175TL*, BL, BR; 176BR; 177TL, TR; 179TR; 181; 185BL; 186TL, TR; 187TL, BR; 188TL; 190BL. (* = designer Annie Kelly) **TRUMBO, KEITH:** 42BR; 56T; 67TR; 69B; 94; 101BL; 109BL; 119TR; 120TL, TR; 121BL; 123T, C.